Si

Roz Austin

ISBN: 978-1-9998638-1-4

First paperback edition published 2018

COVER DESIGN BY ANASTASIA SICHKARENKO

Cover image: © Anastasia Sichkarenko 2018

Jacket layout: © Katie Gabriel Allen 2018

Copy-editor: Brenda Stone

When you aim for perfection, you
discover it's a moving target.

- *George Fisher*

In memory of my grandpa, Ronald

With thanks also to Fred, Cherry, Brenda, Amy and Dennis for help and advice in the writing and production of this book

CONTENTS

FOREWORD

Anorexia nervosa - literally meaning 'loss of appetite due to a nervous or emotional cause' - is a common illness, especially amongst teenage girls. It is likely that you will know someone who suffers from an eating disorder, or perhaps you have had one yourself. A characteristic of eating disorders is that the sufferer often doesn't realise that they are ill. This can be a problem because anorexia nervosa is a very dangerous condition; it has a higher risk of serious complications and death than any other mental disorder. Helping people with anorexia nervosa to realise early on that they need help is really important to help prevent any long-term consequences of the illness and increase the chance of full recovery.

Size *Zero* is a contemporary novel exploring fourteen-year-old Suzy's experience of anorexia nervosa. Suzy's illness is a classic example of anorexia nervosa, and Size *Zero* cleverly combines Suzy's descent into its grip with the normal events of teenage life occurring around her. For anyone experiencing an eating disorder themselves, they will recognise Suzy's feelings, which may help lessen their own sense of isolation. Suzy's story shows how important the support of family and friends is to recovery, and illustrates how best to approach eating problems and help the sufferer during their recovery.

I work as an NHS psychiatrist and have experienced anorexia nervosa myself. Suzy's experiences resonate with me, but she was lucky enough to get intensive treatment for her problems relatively early on. I teach medical students and future GPs about eating disorders and their treatment, and would certainly suggest reading Size *Zero* as part of such studies.

If you think you have an eating disorder, or are worried about someone else, I would urge you to read this book and then seek help from your parents, a teacher or your GP. Good luck!

Dr Rebecca McKnight
University of Oxford, Department of Psychiatry
Member of the Royal College of Psychiatrists
BA (Hons), BMBCh, MA (Oxon), MRPsych

PROLOGUE

The first time I see Tasha at Uni after the summer holidays, I'm not sure it's her. Those eyes like dark shadows, those cheekbones sticking outwards. Her smile makes the skin taut and her face seems far older. Even her blonde hair seems limp. Her tiny purple maxi-dress shows off coat-hanger collarbones and arms that might snap. *Mustn't stare, it's rude.* But last year she'd had a confidence I envied, fitting with ease into the whirlwind of parties, always smart and funny and looking stunning.

We hadn't exactly hung out together. But Tasha had been on my corridor in college, and sometimes during lazy afternoons or late after nights out we'd sit in her room drinking coffee. We mostly chatted about boys, but I liked the way that Tasha put me at ease. She made me feel special. I put it down to that glittering confidence she had, so it was a real surprise when she began losing weight. I thought about saying something. But what? I never really talked about my anorexia. Suddenly Orange Tree Ward popped into my mind. A numbness started in my tummy, just as a band started to play.

Wyatt had told me before I left, "I don't want to see you back here, as that'll mean you've lost weight. And you don't have to be like the rest of us, in and out of these places." That was five years ago, but the memories haunted me...

PART 1: THE DIET

July 2012

I'LL RUN, WHATEVER

The scorching heat of a July day made the grass scratchy under my feet. In the sun's glare, looking around was almost painful. On the sides of the track sat kids from the four different school houses, texting, taking photos and sipping cool drinks. And then from the track came the blasts of a shrill whistle. The brightly striped runners sprinted jerkily along the track. Blue House were shouting and cheering. For a moment it was electric, and then I shut it out of my mind because I needed to find Carla, the Girls' Captain, before the next race.

She and Gemma were doing stretches. Both wore cut-off running shorts that showed off their lean, rippled legs, tanned from long afternoons of athletics. Carla was Indian and slim. She had a long plait and pretty features. Behind her was Gemma, and every part of her was perfectly proportioned: small, slender arms, a nicely shaped face with blue eyes, and blonde hair tied in a ponytail. They looked surprised when I walked nervously up to them.

"You running, Suzy?" asked Carla sharply. She stared at me, as if it's some joke.

"Yup, the 1500 metres. Donna's injured, and she asked me to take her place."

Carla exchanged doubtful glances with Gemma, and then she frowned. "Now we're going to lose," she said. "I can't run. I've got the shot-put and Gemma's just run the 800 metres." Carla knelt down and tightened her shoelace.

"Don't worry, it'll be all right," I said. "I've been practising." The silence was uneasy and I felt my heart pounding unevenly.

"We haven't got much choice," Gemma said. "Kinda looks like we've no one else."

"Well Suzy, if you don't mind running..." said Carla, still sounding uncertain. She took a blue banner from a box, and passed it to me.

I pulled it across my shoulder, becoming conscious of the faces round me coming into focus. I wanted this to be over. I was relieved to hear the whistle again, and made my way over to the track.

My form tutor, Mr Dewberry, was standing there. He was nice but ineffective, and sometimes his stammer made it particularly difficult for him in the classroom. He had a perplexed grin on his face, and I wondered if he was surprised that I was running. "Last r-race of the d-day," he said. "Make this th-the one p-people rem-remember. You need to p-pace yourselves run-running this d-distance, girls." His stammer was worse than normal. "Right, take your st-starting position pl-please." Hannah, from my form, smiled at me. She was trying to be nice. But I knew that she was ultra-competitive, and she and Julie now put their feet into the blocks. I decided not to bother, worried that I'd lose my balance. Nervous butterflies started in my tummy, as I stood there feeling the school's gaze on me. Then, Mr Dewberry put on his sunglasses, pushed his dark hair back from his eyes, and said, "On your marks. Ready...set..." and shot the starter pistol.

I pushed myself forwards and, watching the others' long strides, tried to run like them. I made my strides wider, and imagined my arms were strong and driving me on. My eyes fixed on Hannah's yellow band in front and I didn't let myself look at the crowd.

"Blue! Go Blue! Thrash 'em," a boy shouted.

For the next circuit or two the crowd was distant, and I had a perfect rhythm, different from the other runners, but not out of tempo. Then I overtook Julie, whose hair was stuck to her red face, and she glanced at me looking surprised and annoyed. My stomach rumbled really noisily – I'd only had an apple, forgetting to eat the Ryvitas with cheese at lunchtime. I was desperate for a drink – lots of fizz, with floating chunks of ice in it. My breaths felt shallow, staccato.

The red band was just ahead. The knot of the girl's light brown hair bobbed up and down and I was happy when our shoulders drew closer, then parallel, and I realised I'd managed to get ahead of Julie.

"Yellow."

"Blue!"

"Win, Blue!"

I couldn't tell who was shouting for which team.

Ahead Hannah was running effortlessly, and I got the feeling that she could go faster in the last lap if she wanted to. Then she tripped. It happened so quickly. Her loud cries were agonising to hear. I thought I ought to stop, but the crowd was cheering louder, "Blue! Go, Blue!" Guilt made my face burn even redder. I ran on past Hannah, and on to the white finish line and the white flags.

"That was great, now Blue's gonna win!" shouted Matt, a boy from my form.

I smiled, but I felt strangely dizzy. My boyfriend Nick appeared in front of me, grinning. "I didn't know you could run. That was amazing!" He kissed me full on the lips, but I couldn't focus on him. "Can you get me a Diet Coke? I think I'm going to faint," I said.

"Yeah, sure," he said and wandered off.

I sank onto the grass next to Molly, who'd just dyed her curly hair bright red. "You all right?" she asked. I nodded. She was eating salt and vinegar squares, and she held the packet out to me. "Finish them. I've had a whole bag."

"No thanks."

"I wish I had your will-power. I feel like the lazy one, when you, Carla and Gemma have all done races."

I lowered my head between my legs, because someone had told me to do that once when I'd nearly fainted. I could feel beads of sweat roll down between my shoulder blades.

"There you go," said Nick, handing me a can of Diet Coke. I opened it and a blast of bubbles hit the back of my throat, icy and cold, the best taste in the world.

The others started talking. I didn't want to and said nothing as I sipped my drink. Suddenly I wanted a shower, so I crossed the field, glad to escape the feeling of being watched.

I often went to my grandparents' house, especially after school when Mum was still at work, and I loved the homeliness of Granny's kitchen. Granny was grating chocolate when I came in, and barely noticed me. The blender was churning up the cake mixture for the round greased cake tins, sitting ready. She switched it off, saying, "I'll need a miracle to get this lot ready for the fête tomorrow. Have you got homework?" She turned round, wiping her hands on her flowery apron covered with flour dust and chocolate smudges.

"Nope. Not today."

"Come and have a fairy cake!"

I noticed the wire tray bearing little cakes with pink frosted icing and cherries and iced sugar bits on top. "I've had one," I said, confidently lying.

"Well have another," she said looking at my face closely.

"I'm full, thanks."

"You hardly eat enough to keep a sparrow alive," she said. I didn't want to hear this.

"Julia telephoned ... she has some special news to tell you," Granny said. She picked up her wooden spoon to stir something in a saucepan.

"What is it?" I asked.

"I don't know. She wouldn't tell me. Use the phone upstairs to call her. Grandpa's having a sleep in the study."

As I ran up the red-carpeted stairs, I tried to think what it was. Julia had taught me the cello for six years, an instrument that I was crazy about. I'd won a few silver trophies for my performances recently, although I'd been disappointed in the last recital class when I'd narrowly missed out on first prize. I seemed to hold my breath as I now dialled Julia's number.

"Suzy? Is that you? I've got some wonderful news. You've won a place in the UK Under-16s Young Soloists' Competition. Few people get this chance. It could be a golden opportunity for you."

"That's really great," I said, in a high-pitched voice.

"Could you ask your granny if you can come round and choose the repertoire?" she asked. "Are you free now? I'll come and pick you up."

"Yes, I'll go and ask her." When I put the phone back on its hook, I felt I was floating on air.

When Julia arrived a few minutes later, it was in her vintage blue sports car with a really noisy engine. I got in and slammed the door loudly, without any thought. But anyway, Julia was grinning at me. "Darling, I'm thinking of Brahms as one possibility," she said, her foot down on the accelerator. "But of course it's up to you."

"Which piece?"

"The Brahms Sonata in E minor. I'll put on a recording of the performance I gave at the Wigmore Hall when we get back." She looked at me with bright eyes.

I smiled back, but felt in awe of her. I knew that the Wigmore Hall was one of the very best places you could perform.

Driving fast, she narrowly missed the grumpy judge's car that had pulled out in front. She slowed right down. "How was school?"

"Boring."

"I always hated school too."

Trees rushed past. I loved the feel of the wind rushing through my hair.

A short time later, we walked up Julia's drive. Her husband Michael was mowing the grass near the trees. The pale green lines were immaculate and stretched right down to the stone wall by the road. It was funny to think that a famous conductor did normal stuff like this. He was older than her, with grey, thinning hair, and he walked heavily, his shoulders crumpled up as he stooped over the mower. He waved at us, a friendly smile on his face. I smiled back and wondered if Julia had told him about the competition. I imagined she had.

In the music room, there were gold and dark pink roses and the palest lilies in a silver vase, reflected double in a framed mirror. Through the closed window you could hardly hear the mower, and I listened to the rich chords of Brahms. "Here's some refreshments," said Julia, bringing in a tray with a jug of cloudy lemonade and tall, crystal glasses. "So what do you think?"

"I love the piece," I said. But I was worrying now about the sugar content in the lemonade.

"I think I have my old score here," said Julia. I watched as she turned away to search through the collection of recordings. She was so elegant: slim belted waist, a navy dress with tiny white dots which moved with her, matching exactly her navy heels, and her long dark hair worn down for a change.

I carried on listening. It always felt good in her music room, to be lifted out of myself. Julia smiled at me, and said, "I forgot, you can hear a couple of sneezes in that recording."

"It sounded really good," I said.

"Thanks, darling. It's one of my more special recordings." She looked at the score and tapped her foot, as if she was playing the music all over again. "I think you could play it a little slower than I did." She started the metronome and the silver pointer moved back-and-forth, ticking a slower tempo.

"Shall I learn it for next week?"

"Yes please. You can borrow my music."

I strapped my cello into its case, shutting its different locks. Then the door opened and Mum came in with a bright smile, wearing a maroon skirt which I didn't like and a pink striped shirt that clashed. "So, Suzy, you must be over the moon," she said.

"I guess so," I said. I felt annoyed that my cello lesson was over so soon and Mum would be taking me home.

She picked up the Brahms score and turned to Julia. "I played this in a competition when I was Suzy's age." I didn't know why it wound me up so much hearing Mum talking about her performances, but it did.

Julia said, "Suzy, we'll go with Michael to London if you like, and hear the Brahms played by Stéphane, a former student of mine. I know he's performing it soon."

I brightened at once. I loved nights out with Julia

and Michael, going to concerts and operas. Last time it was *Don Giovanni*. "Can we go in the boat up the Thames again?"

"If you like," said Julia, laughing at my pleasure.

Only Mum's face was serious, still studying the score. She looked across at Julia. "I'll dig out my score too, to compare the markings." I wanted to cringe at this. *Why didn't Mum respect that Julia had been the professional cellist, and not her?*

I was lying on my bed in my room with my laptop, looking up pro-ana sites.

On nights when I had cello lessons I ate my dinner at my mum and my stepdad's house, instead of eating dinner at my grandparents' house. Tonight's dinner was lucky for me. Mum had cooked my food before she and my stepdad, Rupert, had theirs. I had become a vegetarian and so it was macaroni cheese, and I'd found it easy to slip handfuls inside my plastic bag hidden inside my shorts. It was nearly all in there when Mum came in. "Have you finished?" she'd asked.

I said, "Yeah, can I go?"

"In a minute. I wanted to say how proud of you I am ..."

Rupert called out, "Kath, fetch me the Martini, will you?" Mum looked annoyed and pushed some grey hairs behind her ear. I told her that I had French verbs to learn. I couldn't play my cello in their house or Rupert would get annoyed. Just a few minutes ago he'd shouted at Ben for playing his guitar with the amp plugged in. Rupert usually tried to be nice; I think he felt sorry that Ben and I hadn't seen our dad for many years. But Rupert wasn't as musical as the rest of us, and it must have been grating for him to listen to Ben playing the same Slipknot song over and over again. Even I found it annoying. Ever since Ben had started Year 11 he'd been obsessed with the band. We used to like the same music, but not any more.

The internet had loads of tips on losing weight. Most of the girls on the website I was looking at were slimmer than me, some skinnier than supermodels too. Here was a photo of a girl who was older than me, about sixteen, arching her back in her black bikini, showing off each rib. She had to be a size 0 for her to look like that. My goal weight for sure.

The websites reckoned that you needed to feel motivated. Like *litebitetara*, my diet buddy on the site; she needed me to help her stick to melon and drinking Diet Cokes. I knew it would be really lonely not to receive her messages of encouragement when I was finding it hard. Maybe she was online. Yes, she was. She wrote,

Want to do the 3-day Water Diet? No pigging out, not even on Ryvita Thins – ☺

I wrote,

Sure! If I could lose more, I would buy this dress I want.

Wait a moment – what was that creaking? I lowered the screen, and held my breath waiting to see if Mum would knock.

It must be Ben, going into the den where the telly was. I scrolled down.

Tara was writing again.

If you don't hear back from me, it's coz I'm back in hospital... There's a 50/50 chance, so I'm scared.

My doctor told my Mum he's worried about me. LOL.

I was really scared hearing that she could have a heart attack. I didn't know what to email back to her. Suddenly I thought that might not be her real name. Could I die from dieting? No...? I weighed way more than Size 0. But I wanted to wear that white dress I'd seen. I had to lose more.

CAUGHT OUT LYING

Algebra wasn't making any sense to me. At least I got to sit on the large desk in the middle of the classroom next to Molly and with Gemma and Carla. I'd been staring at the sum for so long that the numbers looked blurred in a weird way.

$$Y = X^2 - 5x + 6$$

I was still no closer to knowing how to complete the square. "This is so boring," I said to Molly.

"I know what you mean," Molly replied. "I haven't even done the third question yet. Hey, can I copy yours? Gemma wouldn't let me look at hers."

I glanced across and saw that Gemma was busy writing. She had already nearly finished the sheet, and I felt dispirited. "Sure," I said, pushing my sheet towards Molly.

"Thanks," she said, grinning at me.

"Why d'you want to cheat?" Gemma said. "I mean we have to learn the stuff for the exam."

Molly blew a loud raspberry. "I don't care about that," she said. "GCSEs aren't until next year."

I laughed. I didn't want to think about next year's

exams either.

"Gemma!" shouted Miss Hunt. "Put that make-up away, at once." She looked up from her desk where she was helping the nerd Iain. He was probably doing a more difficult algebra sheet.

There were sniggers from the boys sitting behind us, and Gemma yawned loudly. Most people were scared of Miss Hunt. They called her the Hunter behind her back, because she always wore power suits and dished out detentions for just talking in assembly. I didn't like the way she wore her greying hair drawn back in a bun, and her big horn-rimmed glasses. But Gemma never seemed scared of her.

Slowly Gemma put her make-up away, turning round in her seat to talk to Adam. He was a mate of my boyfriend Nick. Tall with classic good looks, and dark curly hair, he had an athletic build as he often played football. Lots of girls thought he was cute, but I hadn't known that Gemma got on so well with him. She kept smiling at him, and was busy chatting to Nick about the Olympics.

"Gemma!" the Hunter bellowed. "Get on with your work, please! Don't let me have to ask you again."

"I've finished, Miss Hunter," she replied.

Miss Hunter's lips turned into a frozen smile. "I see," she said. "Well, let's run through the answers. We'll start at the end of the sheet, and work backwards. Gemma, what answer do you have for question ten please?"

"X is 9, Miss," Gemma said, smiling confidently.

"Yes, that's right," said the Hunter, looking surprised. "Molly, can you tell me the answer for question nine please?"

This was one that Molly had copied from my sheet. "X is 4, Miss," she said.

"Wrong, I'm afraid," she said. "Any other answers?"

If only I were gifted like my cousin was. Sarah was in her first year of studying Maths at Oxford University. I should try harder.

Gemma put her hand up again.

"Yes, Gemma?" the Hunter said.

"X is plus or minus 2," Gemma said.

"Well done, Gemma," the Hunter replied. "You've been such a chatterbox this lesson that I'm glad to see you've done some work."

No one dared laugh at Gemma, even though she was smiling in a gloating, boffin-like way.

Morning break finally came, and we were standing at our normal bench. The benches were in a ranking order, and my eyes scanned from ours down to where the saddos were gathered at the far bench beside the loo block. I used to have to spend break-times down there with them. I looked across at Nick, who was standing with some of his friends at the next bench, snapping open a can of Coke. I thought how tanned Nick looked, and how I really liked his new short haircut of spikey blond hair. I forgot how tall he was sometimes. He was nearly a head taller than some of his friends.

"What you doing Saturday?" Molly asked me, offering me a crisp.

I saw that the packet was Skips, my favourite crisps. I shook my head. "Nothing much," I said.

"Want to go shopping in Guildford?" she asked.

"There's a new milkshake bar there. Maybe Nick and his mates want to come too?" She leaned closer towards me, and said quietly, "Well, it's Adam I really want to come. I really like him."

Carla replied, "You don't need to tell us that. You never shut up about him."

I laughed and said, "Shopping would be fun."

Nick came over, smiling. He said, "What are you lot whispering about?"

"It's private," said Molly.

"Oh, right," said Nick, grinning.

I noticed Gemma looking over at us critically and wondered what I had done. The look only lasted for a moment or two though. She was sitting next to Carla and they were now both plugged into her iPod. Gemma turned to Carla and started talking in a voice that was too quiet to hear.

The five-minute warning bell rang meaning that break was nearly over. Nick came closer and kissed me.

"Sorry, I've gotta go," I said. "I need to get a book from my locker before class starts." I smiled at him apologetically, and started walking down the path.

"See you after school, Suzy," he called after me.

"Sure. Looking forward to it," I said over my shoulder. I headed towards the entrance to the building. I decided I just had time to throw my lunch away. I pushed the swing-door open, entering the girls' loos, but there were a few girls standing in front of the mirrors doing their make-up. So I walked on to a cubicle, where no one would see me throw my sandwich in the sanitary bin.

A guitarist playing bass rocked on stage. Then the heavy metal faded out, and he started smashing up his guitar. The picture flashed through my mind of it being a cello, worth as much as mine. Nick grinned at me, and said, "He's a nutter! It's not really your kind of music, is it?"

"No, it's quite funny," I said.

Nick's arm tightened round my shoulder, drawing me closer, and we kissed. I really felt the need to draw breath, so I was the first to pull away. Nick now spoke, "Whooaa!...that's some record breaker!" and he laughed.

I smiled at him. *Only in February, he'd kissed me for the first time - actually my first ever kiss. We were at the Valentine Disco, and I'd thought at the time it was a date.* Even now I found it strange that he liked me. His fingers were fiddling with my bra strap, and I worried that if he pulled up my top he'd see my flabby tummy. Noticing the fuzzy dots on the telly, I said quickly, "The DVD's stopped."

"I'll put on some music. What d'you want?"

"Oh, anything. Well, anything that's not rock," I said, grinning.

"What about Travis Scott?"

"Great," I said.

He put on 'Stargazing?', a song I really liked. His fingers ran through my hair.

"Hey Nick, did Molly say anything to you about Adam?"

"Nope. Why?"

"Well, she fancies him," I said, recalling my conversation with Molly earlier. "She suggested we meet you guys on Saturday in Guildford. It'll give her an opportunity to chat up Adam."

Nick grinned, and said, "So you're matchmaking your mates with mine?"

"I guess so," I said, and smiled. Then Nick was kissing me.

There was a loud knock on the door. Quickly I moved away from Nick. His mum, Clare, came in and smiled at us. I liked the green dress and the chunky silver necklace she wore, and her long blonde hair made her look quite young. Clare said, "Suzy, that was your gran on the phone. I hadn't realised that you were expecting to have dinner here with us this evening."

I felt my cheeks turn hot, but I didn't say anything.

"I'm sure it's just some mix up," said Clare. "You're very welcome to have dinner with us. You're vegetarian, aren't you?"

I nodded, feeling my heart racing.

"Is vegetarian lasagne okay?"

"That would be lovely," I said. "I'm very sorry about this."

"I'd love you to have dinner with us, Suzy. Next time I'll cook something more ambitious, and use one of those cookbooks I keep buying but don't seem to use," she said, and smiled.

I smiled back at her.

When the door had closed, I waited a minute or two until Clare had walked down the corridor. Feeling awkward, I turned to Nick, thinking of what I could say. "I'm really embarrassed," I said.

Nick was scrolling through his text messages, and he looked up at me with a puzzled smile. "Why's that?" he asked.

"Well, your mum must think I lied to my gran

about having dinner here," I blurted. "Granny's always checking up on what I'm doing, it's really annoying."

Nick said, "Don't worry about it, Suzy. Mum wants you to have dinner here, and so do I. You know you've lost loads of weight recently," he said, looking me straight in the eyes. "I don't want you to end up ill like my cousin Naomi, who's anorexic. You won't lose any more?" he asked.

"Nope, I promise," I replied. But at the same time I was staring at my arm, thinking that it was way too chunky.

"Have some salad," said Graham, passing the bowl to me.

"Thanks," I said. It was a leafy green salad with chunks of cucumber on top. The dressing was served separately in a tall elegant glass jug, because Clare wasn't sure if I liked dressing or not.

Graham said, "I'm glad that one young person here eats the stuff. Nick doesn't believe in healthy eating, do you Nick?"

Nick grinned, finishing his mouthful. I wished then that my stepdad was like Graham, and you could joke round with him. Graham was like I imagined my dad would have been if I'd known him.

Graham continued, "If Nick had a choice, he'd live on Big Macs."

"Yeah, too right," said Nick. "And loads of fries."

Clare smiled, then turned to me, saying, "Suzy, is the lasagne okay?"

"It's really nice," I replied, and smiled.

"I'm ready for more," said Nick, holding out his

plate, which was already empty.

I thought how it was unfair that he could eat so much and still be quite skinny.

"And I'd like seconds," said Graham. "Suzy, you need to be quick, or Nick will have yours as well."

"I'm okay, thanks," I said, and Clare smiled at me. I'd actually eaten more than I ever ate at home. Somehow I could relax here, making eating easier, I guessed because dinner was fun. I didn't even feel too nervous about eating dessert.

Mum was the one picking me up, and my brother Ben sat in the back of the car, which suggested to me that I was about to be interrogated in the front seat. Still, I climbed in and shut the door; hoping that we could pretend that everything was fine, I just said, "Hey."

Mum waved goodbye to Clare. She turned the key in the ignition and we jerked off the curb. Joining the stream of traffic, the car crawled along, and finally Mum spoke. "Suzy, I'm very disappointed in you. It's clear that you've been lying to Granny and me."

"What?" I said. "No, I haven't."

"Even now you can't be honest," she said.

"I don't know what you're talking about."

"Yes, you do," she shouted. "You know full well that you told me and Granny that you were eating at Nick's!"

"I got mixed up."

"I see we need to get you some proper help," she said. Ben grunted in the back seat like he was agreeing with Mum, which made me feel madder still.

I turned round and shouted, “You don’t have to take Mum’s side, traitor.”

“Well, it’s a fact that you’re looking too thin,” he said.

“I’m sick of this,” I mumbled.

I felt like screaming. But I just turned away to stare out of the window at the shops rushing past us. I didn’t care about what they’d said.

THE FOOD DIARY

I was lying on my bed with the laptop again. *Litebitetara* was online, which was a big relief. I started to type.

Hey, Tara. How are you?

Hi Amy. I'm just chilling. What about you?

She called me by my user name.

Awful. Mum knows I'm dieting. She told me I need help!

I'm hooked on the water diet – reckon I've lost more. What about you?

I started to feel really guilty about tonight's dinner. I couldn't say that I'd eaten food as fattening as lemon tart. So I typed: *I was round my boyfriend's house for dinner, so I'm starting the diet tomorrow.*

Tara *wrote: I stick food in my pockets – or puke after.*

I'd never puked after meals.

Tara was writing again.

You still there? Sorry, g2g – Mum's calling. With the doctor, just tell him you're too stressed to eat. Then he won't say you're anorexic. Good luck! X

Thanks! Bye x

I logged off, and stared at the blank screen of my laptop. I now had a plan. If anything, I felt much freer. Time just to weigh myself. I got up and tiptoed out to the landing. But I could hear Mum talking on the phone on the stairs. Better not chance it. I felt really annoyed as I shut my door quietly.

So I went over to my desk and opened the bottom drawer to take out my food diary. It had a shiny, swirling pink and blue cover, which I loved to touch. The food diary was Gemma's idea to help me lose weight. This was all last summer, when I'd complained to her that I was too chubby: I wanted to be able to wear trendy clothes, to look like the other girls and not get picked on any more. Before the summer break, Gemma, Molly and Carla had given me several little presents in a black stylish bag. I'd been so happy opening them all – the bits of make-up, the navy-coloured nail polish, and a little silver mirror – but when I'd pulled out the present that felt like a book, Gemma had told me to open it later, when I was with just her. Well, by that stage, I'd been over the moon thinking that the others liked me and wanted to help me. Even when I opened this present, the first thought which rushed through my head was *I'm so fat! And all the others think so.* But Gemma had given me a little smile, and I hid from her how I felt inside. *Anyway, wasn't she trying to help me?*

Well, I studied the diet tips that Gemma had written on the first few pages. I did the exercise she suggested and gradually cut out crisps and all sugary food. Now, nine months later, I was several kilos lighter. But I wanted to lose more. I wrote: *Run for an extra ten minutes tomorrow. Throwing away my sandwich now.*

I remembered hearing Molly complain to Carla the other day that dieting was too hard. Carla had told her, "No, it's not. It's about sticking to it. Look how Suzy's shape has changed." Carla had turned to Gemma, and said, "Tell us the diet you wrote for Suzy."

But Gemma shook her head and wouldn't tell them; she gave me a conspiratorial smile.

I stared down at the diary, and decided that I really needed to stick to it over the summer. I may have lost a few kilos, but I still wasn't happy. Mirrors caught me out and made me feel terrible about my chunky curves. But at least I was sticking to slimming foods now.

I love New Look, especially the shop in Guildford; it's huge. I was starting to think that I was never going to get close to the rail where the A-line skirts were hanging. "Excuse me," announced Molly, in her really loud voice, which she'd been training at acting lessons.

A few girls turned round, and instantly Molly grabbed my arm and together we dived forwards to the rail. "There, finally," she said, laughing. "What colour do you want?"

"I don't know really," I said.

"Maybe try purple and red?" she said.

"Okay," I said, grinning.

"You must be a ten or an eight now," she said.

"Size 8, I think," I replied. And my cheeks felt hot, because I'd never imagined that I could be this size.

Molly had the skirts, and we pushed our way back through the mayhem.

"Is that all you're trying on?" Gemma asked.

"No," I said.

"I'm the trolley for their stuff," said Carla, her arms filled with coat-hangers with sleeves and skirts dangling off them.

"Sorry," I said.

But Carla was smiling, like she didn't mind.

Molly said, "We can't spend ages here, coz we want to go to the milkshake place before we go to the cinema."

We joined the queue for the changing room, and I started to worry about what these clothes would look like on. Eventually, we were at the front of the queue and the assistant handed me a black plastic ticket. It was a relief when I could pull the blue curtain shut behind me.

I didn't like the navy pencil skirt clinging to me, but just then I heard my name being called. I peeped my head round.

"What do they look like on?" Molly asked.

I didn't know what to tell her, so I pulled a face. "I think the skirt's too clingy," I said.

"I bet it isn't," Molly said. "Come on, let's see."

Gemma was near her: French plait immaculate, skinny in the strappy pink dress.

Molly stood with Carla by the mirror: both were wearing the same wide trousers and white tops with capped sleeves. "That skirt's fantastic!" Molly said to me.

My cheeks felt hot. *Only a few months ago, they were telling me what types of things to wear to look trendy.*

"Walk the catwalk?" Carla suggested.

I laughed with the others, hearing the aisle between the changing rooms described in this way.

"The skirt looks tight," Gemma said. "I'd give up on the super skinny size."

I felt really ashamed.

"Reckon so?" Molly said. "I think it looks good." I noticed Molly's eyes lock with Gemma's, and she looked angry. But Gemma just smiled. Molly said quickly, "Suzy, you're loads thinner. I'd love to have your figure."

I kind of wanted even more reassurance, but I didn't feel I could ask for it, and anyway I just wanted to get out of the skirt. I went back into the cubicle and quickly pulled the curtain closed. I thought I'd buy the skirt anyway, to make it a target to fit into.

Finally we were walking up Guildford's steep cobbled high street. I was finding it difficult to walk in my heeled court shoes.

"The boys will already be there," Molly said. "Perfect timing, coz I don't want to look too interested."

"I don't know why you like Adam so much," said Gemma sharply.

"Why? He's really fit," Molly said. "What's your problem?" She was facing Gemma directly, because Molly could be fiery when she liked.

"I'd like to be hanging out with boys who are actually fit," said Gemma. "Like Charlie and the other hockey boys in Year 11."

Surprised, I stared at Gemma. But, she'd been chatting Adam up in Maths!

"Yeah, the hockey boys are really nice," Carla said. "We talked to them after our match the other day. They said they're going to invite us to a party."

"Yeah, well they only fancy you," Molly said. "What about us?"

"They might like you...you haven't exactly talked to them," Gemma said.

"Well, we're here today. I really wanted to go to this milkshake bar," Molly said, pushing open the turquoise door.

Nick, Adam and a couple of their friends sat on the big leather sofa near the window. They were laughing, and as we reached them I noticed that Adam's cheeks had turned red. Nick must have told him that Molly fancied him.

"Hey guys," said Molly, then she turned to me, and Carla. "I want one of those frappé things, with strawberries and cream in it," said Molly.

I panicked, wondering what I was going to have.

We queued up at the bar, and because I couldn't really have a Diet Coke here, I chose a vanilla iced skinny latté. I stared at the double chocolate milkshake in Carla's hand. It had big swirls of cream on top and chocolate flakes. I couldn't believe she'd chosen this, when she was so skinny.

We made our way back over, and I caught the end of what Nick was saying. "...Yeah, we're going to the cinema too, to see *Incredibles 2*."

"Fan-tas-tic," said Molly. "We wanted to see that too."

Actually, it was a rom-com film we'd planned to see, and I could tell the other girls were gobsmacked.

Adam was grinning, and said, "Well, cool, we can watch it together."

Molly smiled at him, obviously smitten.

I expected Gemma to look really irritated. Instead she was smiling at Nick as he talked, with a thoughtful, soft look in her eyes. And I didn't like what it suggested. I started to feel nervous.

"I'M JUST STRESSED OUT. THAT'S ALL."

My name's finally been called over the intercom. Immediately Mum got up, still holding her notepad open at the page where she'd been writing her scrawled notes.

"Hurry up, we don't want to miss this appointment," she said.

"I'm coming," I said and reluctantly joined her.

I rarely saw Dr Chaplain, and then it was for something like bad flu or when I'd had measles. I started to worry about what he'd say about me having lost weight.

He looked up as we entered. He was quite old, with grey curly hair; but as he smiled at us across his desk, his eyes looked kind. "How can I help?" he asked.

"Suzy's been losing weight, and I'm concerned it could be anorexia," Mum blurted out.

I hadn't reckoned on her getting to the point so quickly, and I stared down at the desk.

"Certainly you do look thinner, Suzy," said Dr Chaplain. "I'll need to weigh you, I think. But first

I'd like to ask you some questions. Have you been trying to lose weight?"

I felt panicked that he wanted to weigh me. "Well...no, I haven't been dieting," I said. I remembered *litebitetara's* advice, adding, "But if I've lost weight, it's because of stress."

He was looking directly at me now. "What are you stressed about, Suzy?" he asked.

"Well, with the end of term exams... and the music competition I'm doing," I said.

"What competition's that?"

Mum said quickly, "The competition's something she wants to do."

"Is that right, Suzy?" Dr Chaplain asked me.

"I guess so," I said awkwardly. "But I don't want to do ten GCSEs next year." Since music GSCE was going to clash with the school timetable, Mum was arranging for me to have a private tutor.

"Well, maybe drop a GCSE and do nine," he said. He turned to Mum, saying, "It's important that pressure's reduced as far as possible. It can be a contributing factor to problems with eating."

"Have your periods stopped, Suzy?" he asked.

I was trying to think of something to say, when Mum interrupted. "I think they stopped in May," she said. "Suzy hasn't had one for a couple of months."

"Well, it's stress, isn't it?" I blurted out, feeling embarrassed. I looked across at Dr Chaplain, who now had a concerned look on his face, and his hands were clasped under his chin.

"Suzy, what are you eating during a typical day?" he asked.

"Cereal and toast for breakfast. A sandwich and chocolate bar for lunch, and whatever Granny puts out for refreshments, then dinner like lasagne or...”

Dr Chaplain was looking at me, and he said, “Can I weigh you now, Suzy?”

He stood up and came round his desk. I followed him over to where the scales stood. They were rather like our scales at home, but as I stepped onto them I felt sick with anxiety.

“What height are you?”

“Suzy’s five foot six,” Mum said.

Dr Chaplain looked at a chart: “This means you’re 3 kilos underweight,” he said.

I looked over at Mum. Her face looked white and pinched. “So what happens now?” she asked.

Dr Chaplain sat down at his desk again. “I don’t think we should panic. Girls of Suzy’s age often lose weight. It can be part of puberty, but we should keep an eye on it. If she loses any more weight, bring her back.”

He thought that Mum was over-reacting, and I felt relieved.

“Thanks for your help,” said Mum, sounding unsure.

Dr Chaplain smiled at us, and said, “Nice to see you both. Goodbye.”

I was the first one out of the door, and smiled at Mum. “See, I told you there was nothing wrong with me.”

But she didn’t answer.

Arriving late at my form was actually a good thing. But I didn’t expect Mr Dewberry to hand me a sheet. “I’d like you to write down what st-strengths you have,” he said. “And the areas in your sc-

schoolwork and other activities...which you th-think need more effort."

Molly was making a face next to him, and it was hard not to smile.

"What about the school orchestra?" he asked me. "I enjoyed v-very much the solo you recently p-played of 'The S-swan'. It's a favourite of mine."

I nodded, feeling my cheeks turn red. I was glad when he walked away.

A paper aeroplane now sailed over Mr Dewberry's head, getting stuck on one of the oars fastened to the wall. It was impressive to think that Mr Dewberry had a rowing Blue from Cambridge University.

"Hey, I want you to f-focus on f-finishing these s-sheets," said Mr Dewberry, looking at his watch. "You've only got t-twenty minutes left."

Molly pulled another face.

I stared down at my sheet, struggling to think of some strengths I had.

"We didn't get French Club after school this year," said Carla.

"Suzy, you're good at French. You could put that down," said Gemma. Sitting next to me, she was looking at my empty sheet.

I smiled weakly at Gemma. I was glad that she was being nice to me. I now wished that I was brainy like her.

"Yeah, Suzy, you remember the vocab," Molly said. "And you make up good sentences that sound French. I wish I could do that."

"Thanks. It's because my granny's friend Denise is French, and she gives me conversation practice." But I didn't want to look clever, so I said, "Are you going to the disco at the youth club on Friday?"

"Yeah, probably," said Molly. "All of us are."

"Great."

"We could maybe meet before?" suggested Carla.

I hadn't expected her to suggest this, and when I looked at Gemma, even she smiled. But her eyes looked distant. And I wondered if the smile was genuine, or if actually she wished that Carla hadn't asked me.

The group was sitting under the copper beech tree in the field, but no one said anything to me when I joined them. Only Carla smiled at me in a fleeting way and then turned round to look at Molly.

Molly was crying and Carla put her arm round Molly to comfort her.

"What happened?" I asked Gemma.

But she ignored me, and turned to Molly. "I still don't get why the Hunter's blaming you for it, Molly."

"Me neither," Molly said, sniffing loudly. "I mean it was those Year 11 boys who stuck the glue round her filing cabinet for a stupid joke. Then the Hunter blamed me, just because I was using glue on those glitter cards."

I didn't know which boys they were talking about. But after Gemma had been so short with me, I didn't feel able to ask.

"Well, the Hunter's an idiot," said Gemma, taking a bite of her egg sandwich. "And those Year 11s don't want to be stuck in after-school detention, do they?" Gemma fished some tissues out of her bag and passed them to Molly. Then she took a banana out of her lunchbox, and slowly unpeeled the skin.

I felt a wave of envy that Gemma could eat quite a bit and stay really slim.

"What can I do?" Molly asked.

"Dunno," Gemma said. "Coz if you grass on those boys, they'll make all of our lives a nightmare."

I stared at the grass. I didn't have any bright ideas either. Anyway, I'd missed the Maths class that morning where it had all happened. I didn't like seeing Molly cry. She was the nicest one in the group, and was always coming up with ideas of fun things to do. Molly really didn't deserve this, because everyone knew that the Hunter's detentions were awful: she made you pick up loads of litter, and she put you on the report card so that each teacher got to write about you. Molly stopped crying and blew into a tissue.

"At least term's nearly over," she said.

"D'you think the Hunter will call your dad?" I asked.

"Probably," said Molly, pulling a face. "And Dad's already grounded me for dying my hair and getting dye over the towels and carpet. It was permanent too," she grinned. "Still, it was worth it," she said, twining her red hair round her fingers.

"You could tell your dad that it wasn't you," I suggested.

"He's not going to believe that, is he?" Gemma said dismissively.

I stared at the grass, feeling hurt.

"Trouble is the Hunter's also calling him to tell him that I haven't handed in my homework," Molly said.

"The distraction of Adam, I think," Carla said,

then smiled.

Molly laughed. "He's asked me out on a date now. I'm skipping orchestra rehearsal to go out with him."

I grinned at her, impressed that she'd known how to get round being grounded. She always had her priorities sorted.

I thought that Gemma was sick of me, although I was unsure of the reason, so I was surprised that she'd chosen to do project work with me in Home Economics. We were designing a three-course menu. Gemma had out her notebook, because she never wrote in the nasty exercise books the school provided if she didn't have to. She'd jotted down the first two courses we'd talked about, simple things like melon boats and arrabiata sauce with pasta spirals, the kind that came in three colours, because we were both vegetarians. And now we were racking our brains thinking about a dessert.

"D'you think we'll actually make it?" I asked.

"Of course," said Gemma. "There's a week left of term. Mrs Philpotts probably wants to give us something fun to do in the last lesson."

"D'you think lemon sorbet with fruit might work for dessert?" I asked. I was trying to think of something that didn't have too many calories in it.

"Don't we want something chocolatey?" Gemma asked, giving me a bright smile.

"I'd prefer it if it wasn't chocolate," I said awkwardly.

"But I really wanted to make this chocolate fudge cake that I've got the recipe for, because it's delicious," she said. "Maybe we can make two different desserts? I'll ask Mrs Phillpots," and she put up her hand.

"No, don't...We'll make the cake," I said breathlessly. The last thing I wanted was for others to notice that I was counting calories.

Gemma looked thoughtful, and said, "You're not still doing that diet I gave you, ages back?"

"Well...no," I said, lying.

"Coz that was only meant for when you were chubby," Gemma said.

I hated hearing this word chubby. I'd tried to erase from my mind all memories of how I used to look. I looked round to check that no one had overheard us. But it was flooding back to me just how unhappy I was last year about my weight, and how much Gemma had made me think that if I lost a couple of kilos this would be a magic fix. And that the others would start to like me more. It had worked too. I had transformed a bit like a Cinderella from an ugly duckling into someone who shone, who was even popular. But here was Gemma telling me to forget about the diary. I wasn't going to let her do that. So I turned to Gemma as she wrote up the notes for our meal plan.

"The food diary was really helpful," I said, deliberately using the past tense. "Particularly the tips about which exercises burn up more calories, and fattening foods to avoid." What I didn't tell her was that the diary was actually in my bag.

"I'm really glad the diet's helped," Gemma said, and smiled at me. "Coz yeah, it's so effective you now look like you've been on a hunger strike for months –" Her voice trailed off as Mrs Philpotts came towards us. Gemma gave me a bitchy smile, and there was a nasty glint in her eyes.

I felt really shaky, and stared at Mrs Philpotts numbly. She'd just had her hair cut in a bob, and it was nicely dyed a mahogany colour. "So girls, what have you come up with?" she asked.

Gemma showed her the notepad.

"Good," Mrs Philpotts said. "Because you'll be making this next week. I must just tell the class this, before the bell goes."

As Mrs Philpotts clapped her hands, Gemma gave me a triumphant look. I tried to ignore it. If only she wasn't my partner in the cooking session next week.

Julia was sitting next to me, in the plush seats of the Royal Festival Hall.

"I still remember my first time coming to a concert here," she said. "I was nine when my father decided he wanted to bring me to hear Jacqueline du Pré playing the Elgar. Her playing was so magical..." she said, and she broke off. Her eyes looked watery, but she was smiling.

I smiled back at her.

"Here's the programme," Michael said, leaning across Julia and smiling brightly at me.

"Yes, thanks", I said, taking it from him.

I saw that the Brahms Double Concerto for cello and violin was being played first. Julia hadn't been able to get tickets to hear Brahms Sonata in E Minor at the weekend, so she had brought me to this concert instead.

Voices round us grew quieter. I looked down at

the orchestra walking onto the stage, all looking relaxed. It was funny how you could match people with their instruments; just as people looked a bit like their dogs. Mum used to tell me that I had pianist's hands with my long fingers. Maybe that was because she preferred me to play the piano. I guess because Mum had wanted to be a concert pianist.

"That's Stéphane, playing the cello," said Julia. "I taught him until he went to the Royal College. He's really having a good career. He's playing the second desk in the Philharmonic, and he's only twenty-two."

Michael had been praising Stéphane on the way in the car. *I wanted to be that good.*

The conductor's baton was so precise, always knowing which section of the orchestra to prompt. Julia sat back, lost to the music. I was so spellbound that I was surprised when the interval came.

"There's an ice cream," Julia said, pushing a tub into my hand. "They only had vanilla. I hope that's all right."

"Yes, thank you." I was relieved that she was eating one as well.

After a while, Julia said, "What kind of food would you like to eat afterwards for dinner?" I remembered that Mum had told Julia what the doctor had said, and I felt embarrassed. *How could I eat tonight?*

"There's a nice French restaurant quite nearby," said Michael, giving me a kindly smile, "How does that sound?"

"Yes, great," I said.

Michael was then distracted by a silver-haired man he recognised. He tapped him on the shoulder and they started talking animatedly.

"That could be you up there in a few years' time," Julia said. "I really think that."

But these musicians are so brilliant, I thought. I could never play like that.

"Of course very few make it. And there are no guarantees," said Julia. "But you do have exceptional talent. Don't you think so, darling?" she said, interrupting Michael's conversation.

"What's that?" he asked.

"That Suzy's very gifted...I was telling her that it could be her on that stage in a few years' time."

"Maybe," Michael said. "But Suzy may find something else that she prefers to do. I think fourteen's too young to decide. Let me think, when I was fourteen..."

"When you were fourteen, darling, you'd had your first orchestra engagement conducting some of your own music," said Julia.

"Ah, yes...but that was let me see, erm...1950. Many moons ago," he said. "It doesn't bear thinking about, does it? Properly ancient, I am," he said, laughing.

We both laughed too, as did the silver-haired man.

I wondered what Michael had meant. *Was it that he didn't think I was good enough for a solo career? Or was he trying to reduce the pressure on me?* I couldn't decide.

WHY WON'T MY CELLO SING?

How many times had I played Saint-Saëns' Allegro Appassionato and the notes had sung? But this time they sounded tired. All the excitement I'd felt for the past few weeks had fizzled away, and it was all I could do to grip the bow and keep playing. I heard a rustling of pages and glanced nervously across at Mum, who was accompanying me. Then I heard my stomach grumble noisily, and wondered if the adjudicators could hear. The build-up to the dramatic ending didn't sound like it should; it was just thin and dull. Even the last chords sounded flat. Still, it was a relief it was over. I bit my lip, close to tears now.

"Thank you," said the bearded man from behind the desk. All four adjudicators were unsmiling and seemed unimpressed. "Can you just tell me why you played the movement at that tempo?" the same man asked.

"Oh, usually it's faster," I said. "I must have slowed down a bit." I knew that it was a dumb thing to say.

"I thought it was too fast," he answered. "You

speeded up all the way through, even in the passages that are supposed to be played slower. The beat should be like this," he said, his hands clapping the rhythm.

A woman adjudicator sitting to his right had been studying the score, and she now spoke. "Yes, it was like you were in a rush to get it over with."

I tried to smile, but found I couldn't.

The kinder woman adjudicator, with small features and curly blonde hair, said, "I think we should hear the Brahms Sonata in E minor now."

"Yes, start with the third part of the sonata," said the other male adjudicator, who had greying hair. His voice sounded impatient and bored.

I had been expecting to play the rich opening, but now he wanted me to start with the trickiest part of the sonata.

"Ready, Suzy?" Mum asked me.

I nodded, feeling annoyed that she'd asked if I was okay. If only I'd asked for someone else to accompany me. Suddenly I didn't care about how I played, because the audition was ruined anyway. When my bow touched the strings, a new fire was there, and my fingers just knew where to go and my rich tone was back. I didn't even care when my stomach rumbled again, my body swaying slightly to the music as I played. *The cello and me whole again.*

"Thank you," said the greying man, with a look of surprise.

The adjudicators were talking quietly among themselves, and the young woman adjudicator now spoke. "Thank you, Suzy, for playing for us. You'll have our decision by the end of July. Do you have any questions?"

"No, thanks," I said, my voice sounding shaky. *Now the audition was over. My golden chance, gone.*

Mum was already picking up her music, and she had a pinched, disappointed look on her face. I pulled the cello up onto my knee, and loosened the screw at the bottom, pushing in its spike. It made a horrible, squeaky sound.

"Thanks again," said the man who'd criticised my speed in the Allegro Appassionato.

I started to walk across the room, carrying the cello and biting my lip. But tears rolled down my cheeks. Before I'd reached the door I erupted in horrible sobs, the kind I'd want to bury my head under the pillow to hide.

Julia was waiting in the room downstairs, but as I went in I couldn't stop the tears dampening my cheeks. It didn't help when she put her arm round me. If anything I felt worse, because I felt I'd let her down really badly.

"So what went wrong?" Julia asked gently.

"All of it was awful," I blurted out.

Mum interrupted, saying, "She's exaggerating. There were some very good moments in the Brahms."

"Yes...moments, exactly!" I shouted. "And the other piece was rubbish."

"Look, there'll be plenty more competitions besides this one," said Julia.

"Exactly!" Mum said.

"But I wanted to win this one," I said.

"I know it's disappointing," Julia said.

But Mum couldn't even say that! She just had this

straight, poker face look, like her face was made of plaster. I pushed my cello into its case and snapped shut the locks. I didn't see the younger woman adjudicator until it was too late.

"You looked really upset leaving the room, so I wanted to check you were all right," she said.

"That's really kind of you," Julia said.

"I'm fine, thanks," I muttered.

"That's good," the woman adjudicator replied. "I, and the rest of the panel, were concerned because you looked very upset, and, erm... ill. You're so thin."

Nothing had been said about my performance!

"She's got anorexia," Mum said.

"Oh, I see," said the woman.

I felt really embarrassed, and expected her to flinch. Instead, she looked at me directly, with this serious look in her eyes. When she spoke it was kindly. "Well, it wasn't a fair run then, was it? Why don't you enter for the competition again next year, because I can tell that you have promising talent. By next year you could have recovered."

"What a good idea," Julia said, in an encouraging voice.

I forced a smile. *Yes, maybe. But recovery meant putting on weight, didn't it? And that was the last thing I wanted to happen.*

"So where've you been?" asked Ben, looking up from his bowl of Coco Pops, as I came into the kitchen.

"Nowhere."

"Yeah, so why the mud?" he asked. "You've been

running in the fields at the back, haven't you?"

I looked down and saw mud on my trainers and dirty splotches on my leggings. Evidence I couldn't really hide. "So...you won't tell Mum, will you? Please don't," I begged.

"Okay, this time I won't," he said. "But she's onto your exercising. She's not stupid, you know. Everyone notices those weird creaks coming from your room."

"I don't know what you mean," I said. Suddenly I remembered my food diary was hidden behind the bread bin. I'd put it there before I went for my run, as I'd wanted to read it over breakfast. But I needed a shower and couldn't risk leaving it down here, so I went over to get it.

"What's that?" asked Ben, staring at my diary.

"That's none of your business," I snapped.

"Well, maybe it is," he replied. "If you're writing stuff in there about diets."

"You've read it!" I blurted out.

"So it is?" he asked me.

"No, don't be stupid..." I said dismissively, trying to sound relaxed about it. "It's private stuff actually, that you've got no right to read." My voice trailed off as Mum entered the room.

She was still dressed in her white flannel dressing gown, but luckily she hadn't put her contacts in yet, so she couldn't see the mud. "Both of you need to get a move on or we'll be late," she said.

I shifted my diary across to my other hand to hide it from Mum, and left the kitchen quickly.

Later that morning, we had swimming. I followed Molly into the changing room and out to the pool area. I gripped my towel round my waist to hide my thighs, as I hated their dimpled cellulite. Otherwise I couldn't have faced going out there, even though I knew the towel made me stand out. Molly laughed at Adam, who was holding the nerd Iain in a headlock. Iain was desperately trying to wriggle free, and I saw his mouth clenched in grim determination. I felt sorry for him, but Mr Dewberry didn't seem to notice the whole scene.

Molly was looking at me, and said, "You're looking loads thinner. I'm worried about you."

"I'm fine," I said quickly. I didn't want to talk about my weight loss, so I said quickly, "I'm glad you're swimming too. There are not many of us today, are there? I guess that most are at the prize-giving." This ceremony was taking place in the assembly hall, with all the prize-winners from each school year gathered with their parents.

"Yeah, well, I'd much rather be out here," Molly said.

She smiled and drifted ahead, and I noticed that her purple dotted costume had a short frilly skirt. I guess it was to hide her chunky legs. I wondered if I should get one like that.

"Year 9, you're making a lot of noise," Mr Dewberry called out.

"Sir, can we play volleyball in there?" Adam shouted from the pool.

I was feeling really awkward. I was the only one not yet in the pool. Where could I drop my towel and still make it to the pool without anyone seeing my legs?

Everyone was moving into two teams. I dumped the towel and, glancing round to check that no one was looking at me, jumped into the deep end. Icy water sluiced over my head and I shot up to the surface again, gasping at the cold.

"You took ages," Molly said. "I thought you weren't getting in the pool. But now you can be in my team, right?" she said, beaming at me.

"Yeah, sure," I said.

But I hated the idea of being so visible. For every time the ball came my way, I'd have to leap up into the air to catch it, and everyone would see my chunky arms.

I started to wonder if the prize-giving wouldn't have been better. But unexpectedly I hadn't won the music trophy; they'd given it to someone who played the drums. Carla had won the sports trophy for her contribution to team sports, and Gemma had got prizes for both Maths and Spanish. I hated to think of her gloating, rub-it-in-your-face smile when I saw her next.

"I don't know why you girls are on diets," Nick said to Molly, as they sat at the picnic bench. "What's in that sandwich?" he asked her.

"In the Ryvitas?" Molly waved the hand holding her lunch.

Nick nodded.

"Rye, it tastes nice. Want some?" she teased him.

They hadn't seen me. My feet felt frozen to the spot as I strained to hear.

"No way!" Nick replied quickly. "That stuff is cardboard. You'd never catch me eating those."

"Well, you're not overweight," said Molly, sounding pissed off.

"And you think that Adam would like you to be slimmer?" Nick said. "Trust me, he doesn't. Guys like girls to have curves. Actually, I don't think it's healthy the way you girls are always talking about diets. I don't think it's good for Suzy to hear it...I'm really worried about her..."

I came up to them quickly. "Hiya, sorry I took so long," I said. "What are you two gossiping about?" I stared at Nick, feeling furious that he'd been talking to Molly about my dieting.

Nick said, "Oh, just that Molly's erm..." His voice trailed off.

"That I'm going for diet options, which is pretty stupid," Molly said quickly, looking at Nick. She then wittered on about the prize-giving and how good it was to be really average at everything to avoid it. But Nick didn't say anything for ages. Only after the bell went for registration, and we started to walk along the path, did Nick say, "The fair is coming to town next week. D'you girls want to go next Saturday? We could make a group."

"Sounds good," said Molly.

"I dunno if I can go," I said.

"But it won't be the same without you," replied Molly.

"Yeah, try and come," said Nick. He turned round and gave me a genuine smile. I found myself returning a weak smile, even though I was still angry with him.

THE DODGEMS

Coming out of Home Economics, I balanced my cake carefully in its tin as I walked along with Gemma and the other girls. Seeing Nick standing by the gate, I waved and shouted, "Hey, Nick!"

He grinned, and came over to meet us. "This is the best day of the year," he said. "Now we've got six weeks of freedom to do what we want."

Gemma and I both stopped. "I thought you did that anyway," Gemma said.

Nick grinned at her.

I cut in, "We've just been baking, and I thought you could be our guinea pig."

Nick laughed, and said, "You know me, I'll eat anything...well, nearly anything."

"Do you trust us?" Gemma asked.

"I think you're being set up, mate," said Adam, who had come over, hand in hand with Molly.

"Close your eyes, Nick," Gemma instructed.

Nick did as she told him, grinning kind of dumbly.

"Suzy, I need your jumper," Gemma was saying. "We'll use it as a blindfold." I reluctantly passed it to her, for her to tie it really tightly round Nick's head. "Right, that looks okay...promise you can't see anything?" she asked him.

I was too surprised to stop what happened next. I'd already opened the tin, and Gemma reached in and broke off a small piece of cake. "Right, open your mouth," she said to Nick, and pushed in a chocolate mouthful.

"Yum...delicious," Nick said.

"So what is it?" Gemma asked.

"Chocolate cake...with Smarties on top," he said.

"Well done, mate," said Adam. "You should be tasting for Cadbury's."

The others laughed, but I stayed silent. Nick was struggling with his blindfold, because it was tied so tightly. Grudgingly, I loosened it for him. He grinned at us, and said, "So I was right, girls?"

"Well yes, this once," said Gemma, and she smiled across at him before walking over to join some girls she was friends with.

"Do I get a whole slice?" Nick asked me.

"Yes, good question," Adam said, smiling at me.

I still felt really annoyed. "Sure, there's loads," I said, and opened the tin for them to help themselves. Then Nick kicked a football to Sam, and the boys went off dribbling the ball along the road as they ate the crumbling cake.

Molly took a slice too, but she was looking in Gemma's direction. In a low voice, she said to me, "I'd go mad if she did that with my boyfriend..."

"I am angry," I said miserably.

"Gemma can be a real bitch," said Molly. "You should know something else too."

"What?"

"I've actually been meaning to tell you for some time, but I didn't know how to...You know when our group started being nice to you, and gave you the bag with the presents in it?"

I nodded. *How could I forget?* I kept the stylish black bag for special occasions, but also treasured the little silver mirror and of course the food diary. Suddenly fear spread through me: "Why are you asking?"

Molly looked awkward, and said slowly, "Well, the bag and the presents weren't really a birthday present..."

"No?" I said. "Well – Carla did tell me ages ago that the presents weren't just for my birthday, but that you all felt really bad about picking on me, and the presents were a way of saying 'sorry'."

Molly shook her head slowly. "I feel really bad saying this, because now I've got to know you I like you a lot. And I know Carla feels the same way. But the presents were Gemma's idea. She thought we should have an experiment to see if we could change you from being someone a bit nerdy and..." She broke off, searching for the right word.

"Chubby," I suggested.

"I guess so." She continued, "...into someone popular and, well, trendy, by giving you these things. Remember, we gave you tips on doing your make-up, and getting trendy clothes..."

"Is that why you started to invite me to parties?" I asked.

"I guess so." Molly added quickly, "But now you'd be one of the first people I'd invite to things, because it's great hanging out with you."

"And what about Nick?" I asked, in a choked

voice. "Did you get him to ask me out?"

"No, absolutely not. Nick's not like that. He wouldn't have wanted to have been in on our stupid experiment...Look, I don't want you to get upset. I feel really bad now, coz honest we do like you, and Nick's really charmed by you. Anyone can see that. I think Gemma's jealous of you, coz she's fancied Nick for ages."

It didn't make me feel better hearing her say this.

Molly went on, "Don't worry. I've had enough of Gemma. If you don't want to say something about what's just happened, I will."

"No, I'll say something," I said, thinking that things would get much worse for me if I didn't stand up to Gemma myself.

End-of-term celebration! The fair was absolutely packed with people. It was always exciting to come here. We were queuing up to go on the dodgems, and the loud beats of the techno music blasting from the stereos was making my ears pop. I couldn't really hear what anyone was saying. Nick and Adam were getting in one dodgem, and I moved over quickly to a red one, thinking that Molly would get in it too. But before she got there, Gemma had jumped in. Oh no! And she was the one in charge behind the wheel. There was a strange smile on her face.

I thought about going back over to the side, but all of the dodgems were now filled, and there was a long queue of people waiting behind the rope, blocking the exit. Great.

The dodgem started to move and Gemma gave me a scathing glance. "I hope that you're strapped in," she shouted at me, above the booming beats. "We don't want you breaking any bones, because you're likely to if we crash!"

I had been ready to talk back to her, but the mention of my weight paralysed me.

We'd zoomed right into the middle, and smack, we'd hit Nick and Adam's dodgem head on. I felt a terrible shudder of pain, like every bone felt the impact. It was as if I was made of fibreglass and every nerve was shattered. But I didn't let anyone see how much it hurt, especially that bitch Gemma. I wasn't giving her that satisfaction. Suddenly I was so angry I wanted to grab the steering wheel off her. I reached out a hand, but Gemma was smiling and laughing. Anyone would think that we were having fun.

Smack! – it was Molly's and Carla's dodgem we hit this time. Whistles from the boys, Gemma's laughter – I was stunned. This wasn't feeling good. We went off in another direction, and I held on fast to the steering wheel, but my knee was pressed into Gemma's. I was leaning right in with the aim of directing the dodgem to the side. I tried to duck the impact as two boys built like boxers, who Gemma had been teasing, sent their dodgem, wham, straight into her side. But I couldn't, and I was close to tears. I counted the seconds until this would be over. The blasting music was shaking the car too. Everything about this fairground was torture.

Okay, finally I could get out. *Hang onto the side, no one notices the pain you're in.* Pushing forwards and shouting excitedly, the next cargo of people filled up the dodgems. Would the others want to go on more fast, jolting rides? I eyed up with horror the ride with the spinning wheels and the bar which held you into the wheel. But the trouble was that the next ride with the gently trotting horses didn't look comfortable either, having no soft saddle to sit on.

I noticed that Molly was very quiet. Suddenly she looked over at Gemma, and said, "I saw what you were doing with that dodgem. Can I tell you something alone?" she hissed. I had never heard her sound so angry.

Gemma smiled, innocently: "What? Can't you just tell me here, coz I'm hungry, and I want to get some candyfloss."

The others were staring, the boys as well, and even strangers looked our way. Gemma smiled, looking embarrassed. Then she looked for an ally and tried to catch Carla's eye. But Carla looked away.

"Guys, this is girls' stuff," Molly said loudly. "Can you catch us up later?"

"Whoa!" Bitch fight," said Adam, grinning. I hadn't seen him come up to us, and I stared at him in surprise. *Would they fight? I had no idea.*

But the boys didn't say anything. Nick looked quite awkward, like he didn't quite know what was going on, and started to walk away with Adam.

When they were just out of earshot, Molly said quietly to me, "Suzy, why don't you go after them? This is something Carla and I really need to sort out with Gemma by ourselves."

I felt really hurt, and said, "Can I stay?" Then, feeling really awkward, I said, "Is it me? Have I done something wrong?"

"No, it's not," said Molly. "It's something else."

She was glaring across at Gemma.

“Honest, it’s better you go,” Carla said quickly.

“Yeah, get lost,” Gemma said. “Ever since you’ve forced your way into our group, it’s been rubbish hanging out together.”

“Shut up, Gemma!” Molly shouted. “It’s coz of you that it’s like that. You’ve turned into such a bitch.”

“No, I haven’t,” Gemma said quickly. “Carla, tell her that she’s talking crap.”

“No, Gemma,” said Carla quietly. “You’ve turned really mean actually, particularly to Suzy.”

“Well, she keeps on pretending she’s one of us, and she isn’t,” Gemma shouted, and she brushed away tears. She wheeled round to me, and said, “Suzy, you know the two of them aren’t your friends, don’t you?” Her tone was cruel, and gloating, and she paused. “They saw you as an experiment, and so did I...we wanted to see if we could turn a saddo into someone who wasn’t...”

“Careful, Gemma,” Molly hissed.

“Well, sad,” said Gemma reluctantly. But I knew she was holding back, because she didn’t want to risk Molly’s temper.

I could hear my name being called. Looking over, I saw Nick hovering with the other guys next to the food van. I bit my lip, close to tears. But I was desperate not to give Gemma the satisfaction of seeing me cry.

Molly must have seen that my eyes were brimming with tears, ready to leak out. “Go on, Suzy, Nick’s calling you,” said Molly kindly.

“See. Look what you’ve done,” she said to Gemma angrily. By now I was crying, and wiped away the tears angrily. “I hope that you feel guilty, because, Gemma, you should,” I could hear Molly saying faintly.

RIDING HIGH

Nick gave me a leg up onto the saddle. Not for the first time, I worried that he was calculating in his head how many kilos I weighed, and I tried to block out the thought. I didn't want to seem boring. So I smiled brightly, and said, "Where are we going to?"

"We could go down the hill," he said. "We get to canter then."

"Nick, Suzy hasn't ridden Polo before," called his mum. Clare came out from the stable, holding a brush, and said, "It's probably a better idea to stick to the flat."

"I've been down a hill before," I said quickly.

Clare looked hesitant, then said, "Well, Polo's a pretty safe bet. Nick, don't go too fast! Look after Suzy. She's not as experienced a rider as you are."

"Yeah, Mum, all right," Nick mumbled, sounding annoyed.

They weren't getting on as well as they normally did. Nick had been quite short with his mum on the way here. In the car, I even started to worry that he was pissed off with me too. He wasn't usually moody. I wasn't a mind-reader, so if there was something that had annoyed him, I wished that he'd tell me. I reached down to stroke Polo's grey silky neck.

He was a gorgeous horse, taller than I had ever rode, but with a gentle nature. He seemed obedient, which was lucky, as he'd nearly polished off the packet of Polos I'd brought with me as bribes. Once I started feeding Polos to him, he kept looking at me with pleading eyes. So he'd got extra treats.

Nick had got onto the brown mare, Chestnut. She was taller and broader than Polo, and had a white diamond on her nose. "Suzy, let's go," Nick said loudly.

Clare called to us. "See you in an hour or so. Have fun!"

I smiled back at her, and lightly pulled on the reins. I didn't need to do much, as Polo happily followed Nick and Chestnut out to the gate.

Nick knew that something had gone on with the other girls at the fair a couple of nights ago. Maybe he was annoyed that I was shutting him out? But somehow I didn't feel able to tell him about the hurtful things Gemma had said. Molly and Carla were still so furious with Gemma, they were blanking her. Also, I didn't want to admit to Nick that I wasn't as popular as I made myself out to be. The main thing was that the Suzy who used to be the fat saddo had to be forgotten about.

It was gloriously sunny when we came out from the trees onto the Common. I looked down at our town cradled in the valley, the roofs of its tightly packed houses glinting, but not as brightly as the lake or the steeple. The rolling hills stretched for miles until they reached a green-grey haziness that blurred into the sky. I felt pretty insignificant standing here, looking down. Everything that had pressed so heavily on my mind recently suddenly seemed to matter less. But it was only for a few moments that it felt like that, before the same worry was back. This time my anxiety was about the jodhpurs which I'd borrowed from Clare, as I didn't have any. Clare was taller than me, so the jodhpurs were clingy in the wrong places, and I worried that they made my legs look enormous.

Nick's horse had stopped, and he smiled back at me. "You ride pretty well for someone who says they're a beginner."

"Thanks," I said, smiling. I pulled on the reins so I stopped next to him.

"It's lovely here," I said.

"Yes, I like coming this way," said Nick, and smiled. "Look, Suzy, I know it's not your thing, but me, Adam and Gavin want to record some songs together, and I thought that your cello would be great playing the bass line."

And I'd worried that Nick was losing interest in me.

"So will you think about it?" he asked me.

"Yeah, I'd like to," I said, my mood brightening. "It'll make quite a change. And by the way, I don't have to be playing classical. I actually really like jazz – and there's other stuff I'm open to trying."

"I thought I'd ask Ben if he wanted to play bass guitar for us, if that's okay with you?" Nick asked me.

"Yeah, sure," I said.

"It won't be heavy metal we play, I promise," said Nick, grinning at me. "The songs are actually ones I've written." His cheeks turned crimson. I often forgot that Nick got embarrassed sometimes, particularly about song-writing. It still surprised me. In other areas, he had loads of confidence that I envied.

"When will rehearsals start happening?" I asked. "So if I get asked to do other stuff, I can keep those times free."

"Tuesdays and Thursdays, I think," said Nick. "It's pretty much definite."

Nick was smiling again.

Polo and Chestnut were both munching on the grass. But at that moment Polo lifted his head up towards me. "I think he wants another Polo," I said.

Nick grinned. "He's crazy about those...Don't give them all to him. I want one." He came closer, and took a Polo. "You have one too," he said.

Reluctantly, I popped the sweet into my mouth, and felt its thick, chalky sweetness coating my tongue. It made me feel a bit sick. With my tongue, I pushed the sweet up into the space between my right gum and my teeth. "So are we riding down the hill?" I said quickly.

"Okay, let's go," he said.

I waited for him to go first, then when he wasn't looking I spat the sweet out onto the grass. Luckily Polo hadn't noticed, and he started to trot. The trot now broke into a canter. I could hear my tummy rumbling, but the emptiness gave me a high. I wanted to go faster, loving the air whipping through my hair.

"Is that the letter from the competition?" Mum asked, some days later. "Aren't you going to open it?"

I nodded, but my hands felt sweaty and shaky. Over the past couple of weeks, I'd tried to push the awful audition out of my mind, which had been easier than I'd expected. But now this letter brought all the shame of it back to me.

"Come on, Suzy, open it," Mum said sharply. "Or do you want me to?"

"I'll open it by myself."

I walked through to the lounge quickly, shutting the door. I felt sick now. *Please let me get through to the next round!*

Awkwardly, my fingers ripped open the envelope.

Dear Suzy,

There were many very talented applicants for this year's Young Soloists' Competition, and the standard of performance was exceptionally high. After thoughtful consideration, the adjudicators have not selected you for the next round of the competition.

We wish you luck with your future cello studies. We hope that you will support our competition by watching the finalists' televised performances in December, which promise to be very exciting.

Yours sincerely,

The panel of adjudicators for the Young Soloists' Competition

I stared down at the letter numbly, totally gutted. It was a standard rejection letter, just the same as hundreds of other applicants would receive. Not that I had expected anything different, but it just meant that the woman adjudicator's words after my bad performance were now meaningless and empty. *I never wanted to watch any of the stupid performances on telly!*

The door opened and Mum came in. "So, what does the letter say?" she asked.

"Nothing much. Just that I haven't got through," I answered miserably.

"Can I see it?" she asked.

I hated how she was so pushy. Pushing the letter into her hands, I stormed out of the room and upstairs. Now I was going to cut my calories even more. I'd email *litebitetara* for advice, because dieting at least was something I could be good at.

Grandpa was adding apple juice into the large punch bowl. "Want to try some, lass?" he asked me.

"Okay, a little bit," I said, adding quickly, "I bet it's really nice."

"Well, you be the judge," he said, reaching down a couple of tumblers from the cupboard. He used the pitcher to fill them both up and passed me a tumbler.

I took a couple of sips of the sweet orangey-raspberry punch. There must be loads of calories in it, I thought.

"Does it need more juice?" he asked.

"No...no more," I said quickly.

"I forgot to tell you, lass, about an hour ago that nice boy... what's his name?"

"Nick," I said. I smiled, because I could tell from the twinkle in Grandpa's eyes that he really knew Nick's name and he was trying to pull my leg.

"Ah, that's it...Nick," he said. "He wanted to know if you'd be going round to his house before the dance."

"And what did you tell him?" I asked. My throat felt clammed up.

"That you were having some girls round here," Grandpa said.

"You didn't say that I have to eat dinner here at the moment?" I asked. Mum had made me agree to eating meals with my grandparents until I'd gained some weight, or I couldn't go out with my friends.

"No...Do you take me for a fool, lass?" Grandpa said. "But I did say that he could come over. Was that all right?"

I nodded. "And is he?" I said quickly. It was harder getting away with not eating much when Nick was eating with me. He always seemed to want to persuade me to eat more.

"No, he said he's got some chores to do first."

"Oh, thanks," I said happily.

The doorbell rang. "That'll be Molly and Carla," I said. "I'll get it." I ran through the house to get the front door. I was so pleased that Molly was able to come over. She'd recently been grounded, ever since the Hunter had phoned up her parents and complained about her to them. I wondered how Molly had persuaded her parents to let her come to the disco.

I pulled open the front door. Molly and Carla broke off talking and smiled at me. I noticed that it wasn't tipping down any more. I said, "Lucky the rain stopped, now it won't make my dress see-through."

"That dress is gorgeous," Carla said. "I love the lace on the sleeves."

"Thanks. I got it in the sale in Topshop," I said. I

didn't say that it was Size 8 and the dress I'd set as a goal to get into two weeks earlier.

But the anxious look on Molly's face made me think that she had X-ray eyes and could see the Size 8 label.

I walked down the hallway quickly, thinking that I'd email *litebitetara* for advice later about dealing with old friends who were getting critical and too interfering. I just hoped that Gemma wouldn't be there at the disco. I knew that none of us girls had told her about it.

The youth club was crowded. I liked the jazzy song that was playing and looked up at the pretty pink and green fairy lights flickering across the wall. "Aren't those lights lovely?" I said to Carla.

Carla smiled at me.

I'd never been a good dancer, not knowing many of the steps. Nervous, I copied Carla's steps, trying to keep in rhythm with the beat. Molly suddenly appeared from somewhere, said "Hi", and held out some bottles of Vodka Ice.

"Have one, Adam smuggled them in," she said, and grinned.

I wasn't keen, but Molly was looking at me like if I didn't have one it would be a big deal. I felt annoyed, because I felt stuffed from the massive dinner Granny had asked them to supervise me eating. It had included eating vegetarian lasagne, home-made pizzas and all kinds of cakes. I hadn't even been able to hide any. I realised I didn't know the calorie content of the bottle of Vodka Ice, but I still reached for the nearest one. "Thanks," I said.

Molly smiled and looked relieved.

"D'you mind if I go and look for Nick?" I asked Molly and Carla. "He said he was getting here for 8."

Molly thought for a moment, then said, "Won't he find you? I mean he knows you're coming."

A recent song that I'd heard a few times was playing, but I couldn't remember the name of it. I found the loud beat jarring.

Finally the song was over, and I could speak and be heard. "Look, I've gotta tell Nick something," I said. I pushed my way through to the doorway, but no one seemed to notice me trying to get through, so I started to feel panicky.

I dumped the bottle of Vodka Ice in a bin and went on through to the chill-out room. "Oh, sorry," I said awkwardly. Gemma was sitting with Hannah and some boys, whom I guessed Gemma knew from hockey, as they looked older than us and sporty. I really couldn't stand seeing Gemma. She wore a sparkly, strappy black dress and perfect make-up. Her blonde hair had been curled specially for the night and tied up in a clasp. I'd have given anything to look as amazing as she did.

Gemma looked annoyed to see me standing there and said abruptly, "Is there something you want?"

"I was looking for Nick," I said awkwardly. "D'you know where he is?"

"How should I know?" Gemma replied. She said something in a low voice, which only the others could hear, and they all started laughing.

My cheeks felt hot as I went out of the room. Maybe they knew about the weird experiment to see if I could change into someone pretty and popular? It made me want to cringe. Or maybe they were laughing at how my dress was revealing my chunky curves. It was too hot to wear my cardigan over the top, so I'd left it back in the disco hall. I regretted this now.

In the corridor I saw Nick, with Ben, helping him carry a set of drums. It looked like they were struggling. "D'you want some help?" I asked.

Nick put his end of the drums down and grinned. "Good excuse for a break," he said. "You can take my rucksack if you like."

"Yeah? I was going to say she hasn't got any muscles anyway," said Ben grinning.

Nick smiled back at him.

Gemma must have heard this, as she came out from the room with Hannah. "Who's playing the drums?" she asked, laughing lightly.

"Adam is. Our band's going on in a bit," Ben said. "Make sure you watch us." His voice sounded squeaky, but it was too dark to see if he had gone red.

"Yeah, coz they're really good," Nick said.

I was annoyed at both of them for sucking up to Gemma in this way. And I was starting to think that, actually, Nick fancied her.

Gemma and Hannah were both laughing. "Will do," said Gemma, and the boys moved on with the drums.

But Gemma now came closer to me, until our bodies were almost touching. She said, "Suzy, you know you should watch out...or you might lose Nick, coz let's face it, he just isn't interested."

"Shut up, Gemma," I stammered. "What d'you know?"

Hannah giggled, and then her mouth shut tight

quickly as she saw me staring at her.

"More than you do about what attracts fit guys," Gemma replied. She grabbed Hannah's arm, and they went breezily out to the garden, chatting in low voices and giggling.

Then I saw Carla standing in the doorway, and she had an awkward, upset expression on her face. "Suzy, are you all right?" she asked me.

I just nodded, and said quickly, "I need to get a Diet Coke." I went through to the dance hall quickly. I was glad to be in the darkness, where nobody could see my tears.

Molly came and sat beside me on the bench in the garden, and gave me a warm hug. "Carla told me what she heard that bitch Gemma say to you," she said.

"Did she?" I said, my tummy tightening. "I didn't know she had."

"Well, any minute she'll be getting what she deserves," Molly said, kindly. Her eyes looked bright.

"How d'you mean?" I asked her.

"I'll show you," she said. She passed me her iPhone. It was open on Gemma's Facebook page. There was a picture of a magpie in its nest surrounded with gold trinkets, and the comment under it was, "Magpies steal people's stuff. Don't trust that bitch Gemma near your boyfriend!"

There was a made-up user-name, but I could tell from Molly's smile that she'd written this.

"Thanks!" I stammered. But I started to worry that what had happened the other day might mean that Gemma would think this was me.

"No worries," said Molly. "I'm sick of Gemma being a bitch. She has been spreading rumours about me and Adam too."

Hannah came out into the garden. She said, "Gemma's crying in the loo... Someone's put up a horrible message."

Molly was smiling.

"It was you, wasn't it?" said Hannah, a surprised and alarmed look appearing on her face. "I thought you two were friends."

"We were. But that's history!" Molly said.

"But Gemma's worried she'll lose all her friends," said Hannah, "when they see the post. She doesn't know it was you, Molly."

"Really?" Molly said, her voice feigning surprise. "Well, don't believe Gemma. She knows I sent that message, all right. Believe me, Hannah, she deserves this."

"YOU'RE SO FRAGILE, I'M SCARED I'LL BREAK YOU."

"It's great, Brighton, isn't it?" Molly said.

"Yes, I'm really glad we're here," I said.

We were sitting on a breaker to avoid the pebbles, halfway up Brighton beach, staring across at the white crested waves, where people were surfing.

"I haven't told you about the fall-out with Gemma, have I?" said Molly.

My head jerked up. "No. What happened?"

But Molly was having a fit of the giggles. "Sorry," she gasped. "I shouldn't really be laughing, but it's just all got so petty. She emailed me this article about cyber-stalking, saying it's a serious offence. So I messaged her back, and said, '*So's going after other girls' boyfriends.*' And I haven't heard from her since, and I don't care coz life's too short for people being so bitchy."

"Aren't you worried about the rumours Gemma will spread?" I asked.

"Nah. They can say what they want. Look," she said as she took a purple gemstone out of her pocket.

"It's gorgeous," I said.

"I've got another in my pocket. I want you to have this one."

"Why?"

"Probably seems dumb, but I thought you could use it as a good luck charm. So when you're worried around meals and stuff, you can touch it and remember a day we sat here together on the beach, and you might feel happier."

"But I'm happy," I said. My words sounded hollow, and I felt really uncomfortable.

"That's okay then, but keep it anyway," Molly said, and smiled. The boys and Carla were now running up the beach, and Adam was throwing a Frisbee, really hard. Luckily Molly didn't say anything else, but waved at the others. They didn't seem to hear, they were so caught up in their game. I got up and felt a sharp pain in my chest and I was dizzy. I pushed away these feelings, and ran over the pebbles. They dug painfully into the soles of my feet, even though I was wearing thick sandals. I was in so much pain that I wanted to cry, but "Hey, pass it here," I shouted.

The Frisbee sailed towards me in a wide arc, then suddenly dipped down, dropping at my feet.

"Sorry, I didn't get that one," I shouted. I threw it towards Gavin, one of Nick's friends, who we'd invited along so that Carla didn't feel like it was all couples out together.

"Good throw," said Nick, walking towards me. "Suzy? Are you all right?" His voice was full of concern.

But the pain in my chest had grown sharper.

"I think I need to sit down," I said, now in agony. I was terrified that I was going to collapse.

"You'd better eat something," Nick said.

I didn't answer. We sat down on a nearby breaker, some distance from where Molly was sitting. Nick turned to me, and his eyes were sad. "Look, I just want to help, Suzy," he said. "And I'm getting really scared for you. It's like every week you're getting thinner, just like my cousin Naomi did. She was in hospital with anorexia for ages, and even now she looks really skinny."

This news came as a shock to me. It was the first time he'd mentioned that his cousin had been in hospital. "I'm all right. I feel better," I said slowly.

"Really? You're so pale," he said, putting his arm round me. "When I touch you, you're just bones. You're so fragile, I'm scared I'll break you."

"Sorry," I said, thinking he found me unattractive. "I'm really sorry."

His shoulders were hunched. "It's not sorry you need to be...I just don't know how to get you to see you're not fat."

"Suzy? Nick? You want lunch?" Molly was shouting.

I sighed. Granny had sent loads of home-made quiches, sandwiches and cakes for lunch, which she thought I wouldn't be able to resist.

Nick was pulling me onto my feet with both hands. He held me there, really looking at me. His eyes were such a deep blue, they were like stained glass, and I could see seagulls circling in the sky above the others, squawking excitedly. I hoped that I could feed my lunch to them.

"Suzy, you're the first girl I've been in love with,"

he said. "And I want you to know that I'm here for you."

"I love you too," I said.

Usually we'd have laughed to break the tension, but this time there was just silence.

"We can eat lunch by ourselves if you'd prefer," Nick said.

"No, it's all right," I replied.

I followed him down to where the others sat, already eating. Nearly all of the lunch boxes were open, showing off sandwiches and slices of quiche that I wanted to cram into my mouth. But, I didn't dare to eat. I sat down on the breaker, the wood digging into my hipbones.

Dr Chaplain was looking at his computer screen when we walked in, but he turned round quickly and looked shocked, even though he must have seen all kinds of difficult things each day, even people who'd died.

Mum started crying. "Sorry," she said, sounding choked. "It's just – my mother has discovered Suzy's been throwing away her dinners."

"Oh, Suzy," he said, and sighed.

Mum sat down in the chair to the side of his desk, so I had to sit facing him.

"When did you cut down what you were eating?" he asked me.

"I messed up the audition, and didn't get through to the next round," I said. "And I haven't felt like eating much since then." I was in tears now. "But it's not true I'm not eating."

"You're still setting the goalposts very high for

yourself, aren't you?" he said, smiling kindly at me. "I don't think this pressure is helpful. I'd let the cello take a back role for the moment. The priority's gaining some weight."

"I'm trying to eat."

"I need to weigh you," he said.

I got up and followed him over to where the scales were.

"You've lost another four kilos," said Dr Chaplain. He went and sat down, and said to my mum, "I'm afraid that it is anorexia nervosa. Suzy needs to have treatment, because if we don't help her soon there could be serious health complications. She may develop an arrhythmia in her heart, or suffer from hypoglycaemia, which is low blood sugar, or she may have electrolyte problems. She could collapse and go into a coma. Having a very low body weight also means that she may not be able to have children."

"I want Suzy to have help. I don't know how to get her to eat," said Mum. She started wiping away tears.

"I'll make a referral for Suzy to see an eating disorders specialist," Dr Chaplain said. "It'll be a psychiatrist who assesses her and decides on the best course of treatment."

"How long will that take?" asked Mum.

"A couple of weeks," he said.

"But we're going to France in ten days' time. Should I cancel the holiday?"

Dr Chaplain looked thoughtful, then said, "It depends on you, Suzy. If you can assure me that you'll try to stick to an eating plan that I give you?"

"I can," I whispered.

"Good. Because a holiday might do you all good and relieve the tension." He turned to Mum and said, "Sometimes a change of environment can help young people with anorexia to eat again."

It felt strange hearing him using the anorexia word, like I was now a label and not Suzy any more.

He passed me a menu and pointed with his pen to the first column of food. "You need to eat what it says at each meal. For example, for breakfast it says a bowl of muesli, and that's not the diet variety, and two pieces of toast with butter and jam on them..."

"All she's been eating for lunch is melon and low-fat yoghurt," said Mum.

He went through more meals, but I wasn't listening any more. I had no intention of eating this stuff. I vaguely heard Dr Chaplain and Mum discussing a date for the next appointment. *But I could refuse to come here, couldn't I?*

"Well, good luck!" he said. "And if there are any problems in France, please leave a message for me with the receptionist."

"Thank you," said Mum. Turning to me, her voice was harsher as she said, "Suzy, thank Dr Chaplain for his help."

"Thanks," I said, staring sulkily at the floor as I got up.

"I know it's difficult, Suzy," Dr Chaplain said, opening the door for us. "But I can assure you eating disorders are very common and the great majority come out the other side of it fully recovered."

"That's a good choice," said Julia, putting the chocolate into the trolley. "Fruit and nuts is one of my favourites too."

It was fun, the two of us shopping in Waitrose. The trolley was getting quite full now, and I started to panic. The deal made earlier with Granny was that whatever I bought with Julia, I would eat.

Julia encouraged me. "You're doing well," she said. "Now I need to think about what I'll cook when we get back."

I didn't want any dinner, but I couldn't say that. I just wanted to touch and look at these foods, and even smell them, like Jamie Oliver and the chefs did on the cookery programmes I'd started watching on telly. It wasn't for anyone else to make me eat. And nowadays it was more than a diet – it was a kind of willpower.

"What if I make vegetable moussaka?" Julia asked.

"Okay, thanks," I said.

"Or is there something else you'd prefer?"

"No, I like moussaka," I said.

"Jolly good," she said. "And would bananas with melted chocolate on top be all right for dessert?"

"I don't usually eat dessert," I said, breaking off when I saw Carla pushing a trolley down the aisle. She was with her mum, and both of them smiled back at me.

But Julia didn't know that Carla was my friend, and she was saying, "Suzy, dessert's a good idea. I think you know, if you want to help things..."

I interrupted her to say, "Hi Carla." My voice was breathless because I was nervous: it was nearly a month since I'd seen her, and I was worried that she'd comment on the change in my shape. "How was India?" I asked awkwardly.

"Oh, excellent," Carla said, smiling. "I've left you a couple of messages saying I was back. I wanted to invite you over to show you my holiday photos."

"Sorry, I've been really tied up," I said. I wanted to change the subject. "This is Julia, my cello teacher. We've been rehearsing for a concert. So, we've stopped by for..." I stopped, running out of words to say.

"Yes, I'm cooking a moussaka," Julia said. "We're both ravenously hungry. So, I'd better get on with it."

But Carla and her mum weren't looking convinced, and they exchanged worried looks. As they walked away, I heard Carla say, "Suzy's looking way thinner than last time I saw her. It's weird, she must think she looks fat."

Granny walked back into the kitchen with a heavy-looking mixing bowl.

Julia said, "Iris, would you like a hand?"

"Don't worry," Granny replied. "I can manage."

The bowl made a ringing sound as it hit the counter, then some spoons fell onto the floor. Granny sighed, as she stooped to pick them up.

"Would you like some more avocado?" Julia asked me.

"No, I'm feeling full up, thanks," I said.

"She always says that," Granny said. "She only needs to eat a lettuce leaf and she's telling me that she's full."

"That's not true," I said.

The only thing I seemed to be able to do now, which wasn't watched, was going on websites. Even that was getting complicated, because I hadn't got a message from Tara for ages. Not since June, when she'd told me what to say at the doctor's. I was starting to get really worried that something terrible had happened to her. Maybe she'd had a heart attack, or maybe she was in hospital.

Grandpa walked in, and nodded his head, saying, "Hello" to Julia. "Suzy, is the cooking up to scratch?" he asked me, then he winked at Julia. "Does the chef get full marks?"

"It's nice," I said.

"Then let's see you finish everything on your plate," Granny said.

"I've told you, I've had enough of this," I said.

"She's done well, Iris," Julia said.

I watched Granny take the moussaka out of the oven, and to my horror she started doling it out onto plates. Julia was supposed to do this, as she'd made it. "Wait, I can't eat all that!" I shouted.

"Well, try to eat half of it," Grandpa suggested. He said to Granny, "Iris, let her have a smaller plate." He turned back to me. "Suzy, will that help?"

I nodded. He stooped down to the cupboard and took out a much smaller plate, usually used for starters. I watched as he spooned half of the moussaka onto the plate.

"Thanks, Grandpa. I'll try to eat it, I promise."

"Good lass. That's all I'm asking for."

Mum wanted me to help her in the garage. I hadn't been exactly keen on the idea, but I couldn't say no, either.

"How long is this going to take?" I asked, as she passed me another box from the stepladder where she stood.

"I don't know. But we need to find the torch or we're going to have a real problem finding anything in the tent," she said.

"I don't even want to go to France," I said.

"Please don't be like that, Suzy," Mum said, coming down the ladder. "I want you to help make this holiday work. I desperately need this."

I could see dark marks under her eyes, and her hair was greyer than I remembered. I felt guilty now. "Sorry, Mum," I said.

"I'm just asking that you try."

"I will, I promise."

"So, you'll co-operate with eating what I give you, so there won't be a battle every meal?" Mum said. "Then I'll be able to relax." I watched as she rummaged through a box.

It felt like she was manipulating my promise, but I didn't feel like arguing the point. Anyway, I wanted time to message my friends before I had to pack.

"There it is, thank goodness," Mum said, lifting out of a box a torch that was large enough to light up a family-sized tent.

I cringed inside. Already this holiday was feeling claustrophobic, and we weren't even there yet.

"I DIDN'T WANT TO COME ON HOLIDAY."

'What's this – you spying too?" I said, when I saw Ben.

"No, I'm here to get some sun," he said, spreading out a towel on a nearby sun-lounger and lying down.

It felt a relief to be beside the pool, even though it was too busy to swim. I liked the pool's kidney-shape, and its brilliant blueness. Kids were doing handstands and there was lots of splashing and laughter. I'd brought a magazine to read, but I couldn't concentrate properly.

"Did you arrive today? I haven't seen you about before," said a girl's voice.

I turned and saw a girl about my age with a white floppy hat over her blonde wavy hair. She wore a purple bikini, and was tanned a berry colour all over. She wasn't slim, but curves suited her. "No, yesterday," I said.

The girl smiled and said, "I've been here five days." She pulled a face. "It's such a dump. After you've played pool and tennis a few times you've done everything here. The pool's about the best thing."

I'd been trying to guess what her eyes were like behind her sunglasses. "Is there a gym?" I asked.

"No chance," she said, breaking off with a short laugh. "That's the trouble with family holidays, you don't get to do the stuff you want to. My brothers are lucky they're older, so they got to stay at home. What's your name?" she asked.

"Suzy."

"I'm Amber," she said. "Why don't I give you a tour? It takes all of ten minutes, and you'll see what I mean."

"Okay," I said.

I saw Ben dive into the deep end. When his head appeared gleaming above the water, he pulled off his goggles. "Hey Ben, we're looking round the campsite," I said, shouting over the noise. He grinned back at me.

"Who's that fit guy?" asked Amber.

I found it weird to hear Ben being described like this, but then quite a few of my friends back home fancied him. "My brother," I said. "I'll introduce you later if you like."

"Well, if that's okay."

"It's fine, honest."

I'd been thinking that if they liked each other that way, then I'd have a lot more freedom to exercise. Ben seemed to discover any secret runs I went on these days, and yesterday he'd caught me swimming and told Mum.

We'd turned right along the road that snaked round the campsite, and stopped outside a low, white-washed building. "I spend quite a bit of time in here," Amber said, pushing the door open. "I still haven't worked out how to get served alcohol though." Inside was a dimly lit bar which was nearly empty, but at least there were pool tables. "I'll get these drinks. Want a chocolate bar?" Amber asked.

"No thanks, just a Diet Coke," I said quickly. Amber had taken off her sunglasses and her green eyes searched mine. I shrugged, and said, "I'm on a diet."

"You don't need to be," she said. "You're dead skinny."

I pushed my oar against the bank, and groaned. It hadn't touched anything solid, and again the canoe wobbled alarmingly.

"Suzy, concentrate!" shouted Mum. "I'm getting wet."

I glared back at her. "Well, it's not my fault," I said. She wore a long blue T-shirt, covered with dark marks where the water had splashed.

"How are you getting on, Kath?" shouted Rupert from the other canoe. He and Ben were way ahead, so had stopped to let us catch up.

It annoyed me how he was addressing his comments to Mum. It was like I wasn't even in the canoe as well. I could only think that he thought I was too weak to be able to make the canoe budge. This was wrong. I did more exercise than Mum.

"We're having difficulty with getting off the bank," Mum shouted.

"You need to give a good push with the oar," Rupert called out.

"I know that, Rupert," Mum said shortly. She

pushed her oar quite violently against the bank, and then we were moving. I felt annoyed that I hadn't moved it. We both used our right oars to manoeuvre the canoe so that it was pointing straight ahead. "I think we're doing better now," Mum said. "Rupert, we should stop for lunch soon. What about at the next sandy stretch?"

"Mum, you know with lunch," I said. "Can I have just low-fat soft cheese in the baguette?"

"That's not what we agreed at the campsite. You said you would have some paté."

"But how do I know it's vegetarian?" I moaned.

"Because I've told you it is," Mum snapped. "I'm not going to discuss what we're having for lunch all the way down the river."

I stared up the Dordogne River. My throat clammed up, I felt so upset. The banks on either side rose really steeply, mainly covered with trees; the only building that appeared was an occasional castle. A white and black bird swooped overhead, so big that it could have been an eagle, and its cry echoed down to us.

We reached the bend in the river. The other canoe was already pulled up beside an up-turned white boat. Rupert was carrying out the red icebox, and Ben had the tartan rug under his arm.

Mum got out of our canoe first.

"Mum," I said, "you won't forget what I said about having low-fat cheese instead?"

"Don't start again, Suzy, please," said Mum, her voice sounding thin and tight as if she might explode.

I got out of the canoe and followed slowly up the sandy slope.

"We thought we'd lost you," Ben said. "Your

canoe was way behind."

"Well, if it was just you against me, I'd win," I said.

Mum was putting the baguettes out onto plates. I didn't know whether to take mine and hide most of the bread in my shorts, since they had big pockets. But when Mum handed me my plate, the baguette was massive. *An American portion,* as Nick would say.

"I want half this," I said.

"That's ridiculous," Mum said. "That's hardly enough to eat, is it?"

She broke a piece off the end in spite of what she'd said. "Can I eat it down by the boat? I find it difficult when everyone's watching me."

"No, you're eating it here on the rug," Mum said.

I took a bite: the paté tasted creamy and I could tell it wasn't low fat. I took another bite, but I just couldn't swallow it. I spat it out into a tissue.

"Suzy!" Mum shouted.

"It's like eating with an animal," shouted Rupert. "Kath, she's ruining the holiday." I'd never seen him this angry. Evidently his patience had finally snapped. This made me retaliate with my own anger.

"So what?" I screamed. "I didn't want to come on holiday. I got told I didn't have any choice."

"I'm not putting up with this," Rupert shouted. "You're spoilt, that's the problem. We've saved up to bring you on a nice holiday in France, and all you can do is moan."

"Big deal!" I shouted. "Most kids get to go on holiday in the summer. Anyway you're not my dad, so stop pretending to be!"

"That's enough, Suzy!" shouted Mum, and her

face turned white, as if she was really scared.

"No, it's not," I shouted. "My dad was actually clever, and he loved me, unlike you," and I glared at Rupert. He could never be a replacement for my dad, even if he wanted to be.

"So clever that he drank all his money away...Anyway he can't have loved you, because he hasn't seen you for what is it...twelve years, Kath?"

"Shut up. Shut up all of you," shouted Ben. "I can't stand it. You're all as bad as each other." He was sobbing loudly. I'd never seen Ben cry, except when we were little, like when he'd fallen climbing a tree.

I suddenly felt really guilty. "I'm sorry..." I said.

"You're just as bad," Ben shouted. "Why don't you eat, Suzy?"

I stared at Ben as he walked down the pebbles and sat beside the boat. I somehow knew not to follow him, and to give him space. I knew Ben missed our dad a lot, and he had his own memories of him.

"Are you not going to eat that?" Mum asked me.

"No, I can't," I said, staring at the baguette. I'd only eaten a few bites of it.

"Well, I'll clear it away," she said, her voice sounding tired and disappointed. Rupert was staring out over the river. Even he looked upset.

The songs were going pretty well. Ben had borrowed a guitar and I was playing an old piano. Amber was singing, and she had such a good voice. She could remember all the words to the songs, too. Ben nodded at me, and we started playing the Beatles'

'Stand By Me'. I was jazzing up the bass on the piano.

"Thank you, that was great," said the campsite's DJ. He had a bald, oily head and a very cheesy smile. He was introducing the singers tonight, but he didn't sound the least bit French.

Two girls wolf-whistled as we walked past them, and Ben grinned. I noticed that Ben had his arm round Amber's waist now. Amber was wearing an incredibly low pink satin top over her denim shorts.

The plan of matchmaking them seemed to be working well...

Rupert grinned at us over his pint, when we reached them, and said, "That was great. When a girl's as talented as you are, Suzy, I don't know why you're wasting your time worrying about your weight."

Amber was looking at me, and a knowing look flashed into her eyes, but she smiled quickly. Luckily Abba's 'Dancing Queen' broke the tension.

From the windy path above the ancient, honey-coloured houses, we could just see the spiky turrets of Château de Beynac. I glanced at Mum, who was staring ahead as if the magic escaped her. "You don't look like you're enjoying the walk much," I said.

Her lips moved into a tight smile, and she said, "I'm tired, that's all. This holiday isn't proving much of a rest."

"Sorry, I'm trying," I said. "Anyway, you're the one who keeps going on about me eating."

"That's because you look so ill. I couldn't believe what I saw of you in the shower this morning."

"Well, you shouldn't have barged in on me."

"You didn't answer when I called your name, and I was worried. And I have reason to be. You look like a concentration camp victim with all your ribs sticking out."

"No, I don't," I shouted.

Further up the hill, I felt faint. Beads of sweat had broken out on my face, and I sat down at the side of the road. "We'd better stop," Mum said. She shouted now, "Rupert? Ben?" They turned round in surprise. Mum shouted, "Suzy doesn't feel well. Ben, will you go and buy us some ice creams? Rupert, give him some money."

"I don't want an ice cream," I said quickly.

"Well, a cold drink then?"

"A Diet Coke."

"Ben, get a Diet Coke as well, please."

I lowered my head between my knees. *Please don't let Ben buy me an ice cream as well.*

But when a short time later Ben was licking my chocolate ice cream, because I'd refused to eat it and it was melting, I felt jealous. The worst moment was when he ate its chocolate flake. I wanted to eat that so badly, once I caught the sweet smell of chocolate.

Then Mum and I waited behind as Ben and Rupert climbed up the rest of the steep hill to the castle. I was annoyed, because I had wanted to see the dungeons.

Back at the bottom of the hill again, Ben and I went into the kiosk to choose postcards. I found a fun one about canoeing for Nick, and ones of the castle for my friends. I also bought some red striped rock for Nick. I walked into the car park clutching a stripey paper bag with my new purchases inside.

Mum was speaking on her mobile. "Suzy's very underweight...No, she's not eating anything much now, only a small amount of melon and fat-free yoghurt..."

"Mum, who are you on the phone to?" I asked.

Mum looked surprised, and shut the car door quickly.

"Ben...Mum's talking on the phone about me," I said, feeling really worried.

He shrugged his shoulders. "She might not be. Anyway, so what if she is!"

"Ben!" I yelled at him, as he dribbled his stupid yellow football past me. He took a shot at Rupert, who grinned and stalled it and kicked it back to Ben.

I noticed Rupert glance across at the car. *Mum was still talking on the phone... who was it to?*

"Hey, Suzy," I heard a voice call. I looked over my shoulder to see Amber running to catch up with me. "Where are you off to?" she asked.

I was heading towards the pool, and had my costume hidden in my rucksack. But I didn't want her to know that. "I'm going to the shop", I said.

"Can I join you?"

"Sure."

"Sorry about the bad timing last night. You know, when I came round."

"Oh, that," I said miserably, recalling the scene of Rupert shouting at me to eat the vegetarian sausages, as he'd cooked them especially for me. I cringed.

"My family have arguments too, sometimes," she said.

"Really?" I said suspiciously. "Probably not like

ours."

"Yes, we do," Amber said. "It's more peaceful at the moment, coz my parents are letting me do pretty much what I want. We argue about different stuff." She paused, looking awkward. "Look, I don't really know you and everything, but it's obvious your family loves you, especially Ben. I wish my brothers said flattering things about me."

I stayed silent, because I didn't believe that Mum and Rupert loved me.

We'd gone into the shop, and Amber had picked up an Orangina and a choc-ice. "What are you getting?" she asked.

"Oh, stamps," I said. That was when I realised I'd no money with me. "Look, I've forgotten my purse. I've gotta go back."

"I'll get the stamps. You can pay me back."

"No, it's all right," I said, and ran out, nearly colliding with Ben.

"Whoaa...why you going so fast?" he asked.

"Stop telling your new girlfriend about me and my problem," I shouted at him. "It's not public property, you know." I started sobbing loudly.

"I'm not, Suzy," he said, staring at me. "It's just people are noticing how thin you're getting, and they're worried too."

"I want you all to leave me alone," I screamed.

"And let you die?" he asked me.

"Yes," I shouted, and carried on running, not knowing which direction I was heading, my tears blinding me.

My legs felt like they were on fire, but I wouldn't let

myself stop. The water felt very cold, but I liked the silver ripples my hands made doing breaststroke, the sun directly overhead, and the silence I loved. For once the pool was nearly empty. So when no one was watching, I'd been able to slip my towel off at the side and dive in quickly. *Was it forty laps I was up to now...? I couldn't quite remember. Stupid not to count. Now I wouldn't be able to enter the exact number in my diary.*

"Suzy!" I heard people shouting. I looked up to see Ben and Amber, holding hands. Ben asked, "D'you want to join us for a game of boules?"

"Maybe later," I said.

"We're not going to start yet anyway," said Amber. "We have to borrow some boules first."

"This old guy said he'd lend us some," said Ben. "I know it's an old person's game, but we thought it'd be fun."

"My dad said he'd buy us a few beers too," said Amber, and grinned.

"Sounds fun," I said, looking up at them. Then I started worrying that they could see my body in the water, and any excitement fizzed away. At least this was the last day in France.

Breakfast. The sun was peeping over the pink clouds, and we could now see a fuzzy shape of land. I'd never eaten this early, and the ferry didn't offer Bran Flakes, so I was having Cornflakes.

Mum said, "You need milk on your cereal."

"Is it skimmed?" I asked her, as she lifted up a jug.

"Semi-skimmed, I think," she said.

"I'm not having that!" I shouted.

"Keep your voice down, people are staring." I turned to see a man with lots of wrinkles looking at me, then glance away, going red. I noticed that Mum's arm had started to move like she might pour the milk. *Orange juice had less calories.* Quickly I tipped my orange juice over my cereal.

"Gross!" Ben gasped.

"It definitely doesn't strike me as an appetising combination," Rupert said, a wry smile appearing on his face. In the last day or two he had mellowed. He now made his dry, unfunny jokes, instead of shouting at me. I wasn't sure which was worse.

"Well – are you going to eat it?" Mum asked. "Or should I get you another bowl? You can start eating sensibly then, and have milk with your cereal like we're all having. Semi-skimmed I can promise you isn't fattening."

"No, I want this," I said.

"Was your cabin comfortable last night, Kath?" Rupert asked, changing the subject.

But Mum's eyes were fixed on my bowl, as she replied, "I didn't get much sleep, Rupert, as I was worried about Suzy." They had slept in separate cabins as Mum had insisted on sleeping in a cabin with me. She wanted to keep an eye on me, because I kept fainting. I was sick of having her watch me all the time.

Ben was spreading honey with a knife over his toast, and my tummy churned loudly as I felt the gnawing emptiness inside me again.

I put my spoon down and stared out of the porthole. I could see the brilliantly white cliffs of Dover now, jagged against the pinky skyline, not so far away. England was waiting for us. But I didn't know what coming home meant: maybe doctors weighing me, people's stares, more people nagging me to eat.

Scary.

ONE LAST CHANCE

I sat on the low cream sofa in the psychiatrist's office. Dr Avery sat opposite me in her pink short-sleeved top, white trousers and matching white shoes. She looked pretty sure of herself. She was very suntanned, too. The wallpaper was covered with daffodils that looked like golden trumpets, and I wanted to be swallowed up by one.

Dr Avery looked up and said, "I'm afraid that Suzy is severely underweight."

Tears started to run down Mum's face, and Dr Avery passed her the box of tissues. I just sat there, frozen to the sofa. So, the secret runs round the block, the press-ups and sit-ups in my bedroom had worked, shrinking the flab.

Dr Avery turned to Mum. "Suzy needs to stick to an eating plan from now on," she said. "You need to decide what Suzy has at meals. It's too difficult for her to decide what she eats."

"I've tried," Mum said. "But really it's very difficult to make Suzy eat anything."

Dr Avery turned to me, and said, "Suzy, if this is

the case, I think that I've got no choice but to admit you to hospital. Don't worry. In Orange Tree Ward there are other girls who have similar problems with eating."

"Please don't admit me! I don't want to be stuck in a hospital with anorexics. I want to go home!" I begged. Hot, stinging tears started to roll down my cheeks, as the full horror of what she was saying slowly dawned on me.

"But your Mum needs to feel confident that you're going to eat the food that she gives you," Dr Avery said.

"I'll give her one last chance, that's if she promises to cooperate," Mum said.

Dr Avery started talking Mum through the meal plans, but their voices sounded very far away.

I stared through the window at the birds pecking at food on their special table. Rain had started falling in bucket loads, and I almost wished that I was outside so I could breathe in the fresh scent.

"Well, Suzy," said Dr Avery, "your Mum and I have discussed a diet that I'd like you to follow over the next week. If you eat everything I have recommended, I'd expect you to gain a kilo."

"A kilo!" I blurted out.

"Yes," Dr Avery responded. "You have to start gaining weight, or I'll need to admit you as an emergency." She turned to my mum: "Suzy's weight is dangerously low. She could collapse and go into a coma. She could even die."

I saw that my mum was crying. I wanted to go home, so I stayed quiet and stared blankly out of the window.

"Kath, are you willing for you and your family to

see a psychologist together?" Dr Avery asked my mum.

"Yes, of course," she replied.

Dr Avery went on, "It's important that Suzy feels supported at mealtimes, and that we explore any issues which may have led to her losing weight."

Why wasn't she asking me? I hated being talked about like this.

"The therapy will take place on an outpatient basis if Suzy gains weight," said Dr Avery. "Otherwise it will happen at the clinic, as part of the therapeutic programme."

I looked at her with horror.

Nick had invited me to Graham's 50th birthday disco. We were sitting on a bench, just as it was before my holidays. But everything was different. First off, I was terrified about eating the lasagne. I knew that Clare had made it especially for me, so I would be expected to eat it.

"That postcard you sent me was hilarious," Nick said.

"Which one?" I said, still lost in my thoughts.

Nick looked taken aback. "The postcard of everything that can go wrong when you go canoeing."

"Oh that," I said, giggling. I pushed the cheesy topping of the lasagne under the knife, hiding it. But I was unlucky again. Clare had noticed. Mum must have asked her to watch me eat.

"Suzy, why don't you try and eat some more lasagne?" Clare asked, her voice soft, almost pleading with me.

I picked up my knife and fork again, and took

another small bite.

"Nick, can you get us some drinks?" Clare asked him. She gave him some money, and Nick took the orders.

When it was my turn, I said, "A Diet Coke please. Lots of ice, but no lemon." I had got it into my head in the past week that even a slice of lemon had too many calories in it.

Thinking that two mouthfuls of lasagne was enough of an effort, I lay down my fork, but Clare had noticed.

"You need to try, Suzy," she said. "No one wants you to go away to the clinic, and you'll have to if this carries on..." Her voice trailed off.

Fear welled up inside me, and I stammered, "I won't have to, will I?"

"I don't know," Clare replied, and her eyes glistened with tears. "Sorry, Suzy," she said. "It's just you're not the first girl I've known to get anorexia. It happened to my niece Naomi, too. It's a dreadful illness..." and she went quiet. Then she decided to encourage me: "That's why I want you to get the right help, so that you can get better. I'm really worried about you, and I know I'm not the only one. Nick is worried too..." We both looked over to Nick bringing a tray of drinks for us.

I grabbed the moment to dodge away from Clare, leaving my plate with the cheesy topping hidden under my knife. Whitney Houston's 'I Will Always Love You' was playing in the background. "Let's dance," I said to Nick, grabbing his hand and pulling him in the direction of the dance floor.

It was less busy now, and Graham waved at us, grinning. "I'm glad that my choice of music hasn't put the two of you off," he said. "The pair of you can show the rest of them how to dance," he said, gesturing towards the other older people.

I was glad that it was fairly dark, apart from the disco lights wheeling over our faces, as I didn't want anyone seeing my body which I hated now. I'd tried to hide it under a floaty cardigan and a dark, loose dress.

But Nick seemed oddly frozen in my arms, as if he didn't want to get close to me. Feeling really self-aware, I moved towards him, placing my hand gently on his shoulder. It had got to the cheesy moment in the song, and his other hand circled my waist, and that was when his whole body stiffened.

A wave of panic rolled over me. I tried at first to hold the panic tight inside me, but I couldn't. "Nick, d'you still like me, as in 'want to be with me'?" I asked, my voice faltering.

He didn't answer at first, and I couldn't read his face, which was nearly hidden in the darkness. "I think so..." he stammered. "But Suzy, you've become just bones...and I'm finding it, I don't know, difficult. You really don't seem to want to put on weight."

"I'm trying," I said, my voice really choked.

"How? Tonight you didn't eat much," he said, sounding really upset. "Look, I don't know what to say or do. And you're not making it easy."

"Sorry, I really am," I said quickly. "But please don't give up on me."

The song was coming to its climax, and I clung onto him, somehow wanting things to be all right. He felt distant, but he was still here, and his lips kissed my head. In that moment, I told myself that things had to change, they really did, *because I couldn't lose Nick as well!*

Being at school felt weird; everything was slipping away from me.

I waited in the lobby, listening to the loud hum of voices coming from the form-room. I straightened my size 0 navy skirt one last time. I was worried, because I'd fastened it with safety pins so it wouldn't slip beneath my knees. I wanted to run away, but knew that I had to go in. Taking a deep breath, I pushed the door wide open.

The voices died away, and when they started again they were more hushed. I looked around anxiously for a seat. Molly waved to me and called out, "Come and sit with us."

I hurried over, grateful to slip into the chair in the corner, away from peering eyes.

Mr Dewberry clapped his hands together. "Quiet, ev-everyone. I want to c-call the register." His stammer was worse than normal. I wondered if it was because of the way I looked. This may not have been a crazy thought, because when Mr Dewberry got to my name he had real difficulty saying, "S-S-Suzy." But, no one laughed, no one even smiled. I wanted to run out of there. But I had to wait out the register, not wanting a detention.

The register finally over, Mr Dewberry said, "There's an as-s-sembly in the G-great hall. So c-can you all m-make your way over there."

The others were already moving to the door, and I followed them. But as I reached the door, Mr Dewberry was calling, "S-s-suzy." I pulled a face that only Molly and Carla could see.

I went back into the classroom, and as I did, Mr Dewberry turned to the doorway and said, "Girls we d-don't need an audience."

"We'll wait for you outside," Molly said, and both she and Carla looked sympathetically towards me.

Mr Dewberry shut the door. He turned to me with a concerned look, and said, "S-s-suzy, your m-mother phoned to explain what's been happening. I'm v-very sorry to hear, so is Miss H-hunt. She's h-hoping you'll have lunch with her t-today."

"But Sir, I don't like eating in front of people," I said quickly, feeling panicky now.

"Sorry, Suzy. The arrangement's already been made," he replied. "Your mum wants someone to be with you when you're eating lunch."

Yeah, someone to watch me! I thought angrily as I went to join the others.

Lunchtime. The Hunter's collared me in the corridor. She was smiling, which was scary, as she never smiled. "Suzy, I've been looking for you," she said.

There was a long, awkward pause.

The Hunter went on. "We were supposed to be having lunch together."

I didn't say anything. Silence seemed like the best option.

"Suzy, can I have a chat with you? Let's go into this classroom," the Hunter said.

I followed her into the room on the right. She pulled out a chair for me to sit on, and she perched on the table. She seemed too nervous to sit down properly. "Suzy, everyone's very worried about you," she said. “You’ve lost an enormous amount of weight.”

“I’m fine,” I said. My face felt hot.

She looked dazed. Finally, she said, “What am I supposed to tell your mum? Suzy, she phoned me specially to ask me to check that you ate the lunch she packed for you.”

“Just tell her that I ate it at break, as I was hungry,” I said. I didn’t see that as a total lie, because I’d been ravenous then, as I was now. I just wasn’t going to give in.

“The trouble, Suzy, is that I don’t think that she’ll believe what you say,” replied the Hunter. “I’m not sure if I do.”

“Well, you should,” I said quickly. My bottom lip started to quiver, and I couldn’t stop the tears rolling down my cheeks.

There was a noise outside, and I saw Ben poking his head round the door. “All right, Sis?” he asked me.

I nodded, and took the tissues that the Hunter passed me.

“So, have you eaten what you’re meant to?” Ben asked me.

“Yeah, course,” I said quickly.

But the Hunter was shaking her head, for Ben to see.

Mum was going to be furious when she heard about lunch!

The shadowy shapes were closing in on me, and I could feel something gripping my wrist tight. “Get off!” I screamed.

"Shush...I didn't mean to wake you," I heard Mum saying.

"Let go," I mumbled, and I dragged my arm back under the covers, and my other hand rubbed it. My whole body was trembling. I'd forgotten that Mum was sleeping next to me, because she said she was worried. "What were you doing?" I asked her.

"I couldn't hear you breathing," Mum said, her voice faltering. "So I had to check your pulse."

I then remembered that Mum had trained as a nurse. Had she known girls who had died of anorexia? I tried to picture a dead body, stiff and lifeless. *Was I going to die? It was a very scary thought.* I'd better ask Mum.

But when I looked over, I saw that she'd rolled across and her breathing was heavy and muffled. I thought that she might be sobbing into her pillow; or was she snoring? I couldn't tell. Worry started to roll around my mind. *Was it too late to be helped? Did I want help? I didn't know, and I wasn't sure if I cared.*

Lunchtime. Coming out of the toilet cubicle, I saw with relief that I was now alone. I stopped in front of the mirror, and washed my hands, drying them quickly on a blue towel. For a moment I saw a pale, drawn, skeletal girl staring back at me. The mirror surely teased me? And then fat Suzy was back.

I felt a sudden burst of anger. Slipping my hand under my shirt, I pinched the flesh between my ribs; then dug my hand into the hollow bone around my hipbone, measuring the space with my fingers. Then I tried to measure the gap between the waistband of my skirt and my tummy...three fingers, or was it three-and-a-half? I wanted the gap to be four fingers.

But it was my fat face which bothered me most, and I now sucked in my cheeks. I wanted these to be high, beautifully sculptured cheekbones like models had.

"Suzy, are you all right?" Molly asked me.

I hadn't seen her walk in, and her curious eyes locked with mine in the mirror. "I'm fine," I said. Quickly I opened my bag to find my make-up, and started applying mascara. But then I glanced at her again, and realised that it was a look of alarm that I saw on her face.

Molly had come closer, and hugged me. "Look, Suzy, I'm really worried about you. So are the others. Please let me know what we can do to help. We want to help."

Shivers ran down my spine as I thought about the others gossiping about me behind my back.

Molly said, "If we'd known this would happen, we'd never have said anything..." She looked really upset and said, "Sorry, it's just that I feel so bad that this has happened." She pulled out a tissue and dabbed at her eyes.

"It doesn't matter," I said, my throat tight. "I'd have gone on a diet anyway."

"Well, you're really thin now," said Molly quickly. "You need to put some weight on. Promise us you'll do that. Please!" Her eyes pleaded with mine.

"Yeah, sure," I said quickly. "I've got to go. My mum's picking me up to take me to an appointment at a hospital." I started to feel anxious, as no part of me wanted to put on weight.

"Are you nervous about going to the hospital?" Molly asked me.

It took me a few moments to think of something to say. "No...what for? It's just to get weighed." But I now remembered that Mum had told me that the appointment was going to be on a ward this time, and not at the outpatients' office.

"Well, good luck," said Molly. Then she hugged me.

I put on my brightest smile to say "goodbye" as I went out the swing-door.

Outside it felt chilly, and as I walked past the red brick building I had a sudden moment of alarm - would things change?

The car was parked beside the gates on the double yellow lines, and coming closer I saw the heads of Mum and Rupert. What was he doing there? I got in.

"You're late," Mum snapped.

"Sorry," I said, fastening my seatbelt.

"Here's a sandwich," she said, passing it over as Rupert fumbled with the Sat-Nav.

"But it's white bread," I said, staring with alarm at the prawns and mayo inside. If only I'd eaten Ryvitas with a scraping of soft cheese in front of the Hunter.

The car bounced off down the road, as we headed for the hospital. My throat felt choked up. *Please don't let things change!*

PART 2: ORANGE TREE WARD

September 2012

"SORRY, SUZY, IT'S FOR THE BEST."

Mum stood behind me when the gate clicked open.

"You go in first," she said.

I walked through and stared up at the tall, grey, barn-shaped modern building. I wasn't expecting the windows to have curtains. I had imagined prison bars. The stone wall was mostly hidden by tall trees. Long shadows stretched across the lawn.

"What trees are those?" I asked Mum.

"Orange trees," she said. "They say that when you've finished treatment here you'll be eating oranges."

She seemed to think this was good. To me, they were the spookiest things of all. "It looks haunted," I said. I had to say something to make Mum realise that I thought the place looked really bad.

"Don't be silly", she told me. "How many Diet Cokes did you drink this morning to give you such a vivid imagination?"

"Only one or two. But it's not that," I muttered.

We walked round the side of the building to the entrance. I felt sick as she rang the bell.

The door opened, and a podgy woman with a brown bob and a stern face looked at us. "You must be Suzy and Mrs Reynolds. Nice to meet you both. I'm Penny, the senior nurse."

"Call me Kath," Mum said quickly.

"Hi," was all I said, for I really didn't want to be taken off by Penny while Mum stayed downstairs with Dr Avery.

The stairs went round to the left. The air smelt lemony and didn't let you forget that this was a ward.

Penny said, "It's this door. Wait, I need to unlock it."

She took a big bunch of keys out of her pocket, but she knew the right one straightaway. I followed her into a square room that had nothing in it except for a desk and a chair. Looming in front of the window were some scales, with a white bar hanging over the top of a black platform. A big mirror reflected the scales. To me the room felt claustrophobic.

"Can you take off your clothes?" Penny said. "Leave just your bra and knickers on."

This was embarrassing. "I don't want to get weighed," I said.

Penny turned round, with a slight smile on her face, and lowered her clipboard. "Why's that, Suzy?"

"I don't like people seeing my weight."

"Well, you don't have to look."

I stared at her.

"We need to know what the position is. Come

on."

My fingers fumbled with the button of my skirt, and then I pulled it over my head and dumped it onto a chair. As I balanced precariously, pulling off my tights and shoes, I was scared of what the scales might say. I didn't pick up the tights.

"Onto the scales, please."

I stepped up, and as I watched her chubby fingers move the counter along the bar, I regretted doing it. *The bar stretched nearly as wide as my arms would if they were stretched out. The bar stretches and stretches and becomes an aeroplane's wings to fly me out of here. I crash through the open window and, hearing the noise, Mum and Dr Avery together downstairs go running out into the garden. "Suzy, come back! You need help!" they shout.*

"No, I'm fine", I shout. I smile and wave. Then my plane starts climbing into the air.

"You've lost another kilo since Dr Avery weighed you last week," said Penny.

I was smiling. The push-ups and other exercises in my room had paid off. Even the avocados I'd eaten hadn't made me gain.

"Do you know what this means?" asked Penny, carefully studying my face.

Slowly the consequences dawned on me, as I recalled what Dr Avery had said: that if I didn't start to gain weight, I might be hospitalised. My stomach knotted tighter, so that its hollowness became a cramp. "You can't admit me," I said, barely able to speak the words.

Penny said, "I'm afraid I've got no choice. You're very underweight, and you've lost more since last week. Do you understand how serious this is? We can't let this dieting go on, as it's very dangerous."

"But I'm not anorexic. I can eat."

"So why have you lost more...hum? Knowing this could happen?"

I couldn't think of a good answer.

"You can get down from the scales now," she said.

My clothes felt like a shield when I put them back on, though I couldn't get what she'd said out of my mind.

"Do you think you look fat?" she asked.

I caught sight of myself in the mirror, and mumbled, "Yes." I was staring at my tummy.

Penny had moved towards me, so that she was nearly parallel now. "But you're very underweight. Can't you see that? Look, I'm much bigger than you are."

I stared at her body next to mine. But I couldn't tell her that, as it would be rude.

"When you're ready, come downstairs," she said quietly. "I'll see you down there."

I picked up my tights and shoes and sat on a chair to put them on. I didn't want to go back down. Time seemed to stop. I knew that what would soon happen was bad. This was my moment of calm before it took place.

Slowly I got up and went out. I stopped near the bottom of the stairs, and listened, but the voices coming from the room were just mumbles. I crept closer, my shoes creaking noisily on the polished floor. I still couldn't hear. Finally I gave up and pushed the door open.

"She's already at a critical weight, I'm afraid," said Dr Avery, addressing Mum. "Suzy may say that she'll eat, and the intention may be there to try, but if you take her home it's very likely that she'll refuse to eat the food you give her, or even hide it. The best option is that we help Suzy with the re-feeding programme we have here on the ward."

"Yes," said Penny. "And there's the advantage that here we have other girls who also have problems with eating. So they understand what Suzy's going through, as they have faced the same issues."

"Mum, don't listen to them," I shouted.

"Sorry, Suzy. I don't know how to get you to eat any more," said Mum. "And Dr Avery and Penny can help you." Her voice trailed off. She took off her glasses, wiping her eyes with a tissue.

"Let's go through to the kitchen," said Penny in a gentler voice.

I felt in a daze as I followed them through to the hall and into a blue kitchen, with vases of daffodils on the windowsill and a long white kitchen table. The voices of Dr Avery and my mum were blurred. I fixed my eyes on the curtain rail.

I felt I'd shrunk to a tiny dot.

Suddenly everything grew distinct again, and my heart was thumping. I heard Rupert say, "Where d'you want these?" He had entered through a back door, carrying two large suitcases. *Where had he got those? Then it clicked that they must have been hidden in the boot of the car.* "Kath, what about here?" he asked her.

"Oh, put them anywhere there, Rupert," said Mum, sounding annoyed.

"You can't visit for the first few days," said Dr Avery. "But you can ring Suzy in a couple of days and write to her. You can always phone the ward to find out how she is."

"We welcome parents' involvement in their children's recovery," said Penny firmly. "I think the best thing is to leave Suzy now to settle in."

Mum walked over towards me. "We'll see each other in a few days. This isn't for long, just until you get better." She stretched her arms out to hug me, but I pulled away. "Suzy, please give me a kiss. Remember it's my birthday today. Then I'll have something nice to remember this day by." For a moment I felt guilty, and then the other feelings came rushing back.

"No, I hate you!" I shouted.

Mum was walking away from me, and she was crying. Rupert was already halfway out of the door and he turned and said, "Sorry, Suzy, it's for the best."

I had never felt so alone.

The blackbird looked at me again, as if I might have some bread for him. He was getting nearer. I kept very still, as I didn't want him to fly away. I thought of the blackbird that visited Grandpa most afternoons. Probably, Grandpa was sitting in the garden on his bench right now, sipping his tea, watching that other blackbird. Tears welled up in my eyes. *When was I going to see Grandpa again?*

"Dinner's ready!" a girl's voice called.

I looked up to see an older Chinese girl, with large brown eyes and a dark ponytail. She wore jeans and a blue jumper with white stripes on it. "I'm not hungry," I said.

"You have to eat here, even if you aren't hungry.

And Fran gets angry if people are late for meals. By the way, I'm Yun." She smiled, making dimples appear in her cheeks. This surprised me, as I thought that chubby people had dimples, not anorexics.

"I'm Suzy," I said.

"I know," she said, smiling at me. "We're going to be roommates."

I got up from the stone step and went to join her by the door. "What time is it?" I asked.

"Six. Dinner's always at six here. Everything here is timetabled. It's like my boarding school was," she said, and pulled a face. "The only thing we don't have is bells."

We entered the kitchen, and I saw a young woman with auburn, curly hair drop potato waffles onto plates. After custard, potato was my most hated food in the world, and I found just its smell was revolting. She smiled across at me and said, "Hello, Suzy. I'm Fran, one of the nurses here."

Fran smiled, and said, "You haven't been introduced to anyone yet, have you? Everyone, this is Suzy. I'll leave you to introduce yourselves."

I stared across at the table, around which a group of young people sat.

Fran asked, "Can those of you on the bench move along to make room for Suzy, please?"

My cheeks felt hot as I walked round the table and sat down, next to the only boy. *I hadn't thought that boys got anorexia!* He said, "I'm Wyatt. Excuse the others for being rude and not introducing themselves. When did you get here?"

"This afternoon," I said. I realised that he reminded me of my cousin Jonathan, with his dark, curly hair, dark eyebrows and olive skin. Only his face looked much thinner, his cheeks hollowed out. *Was he a patient, or sent there to spy on us? Sitting next to me, he could report everything I didn't eat to Penny.* I stared as a plate of waffles and baked beans was put down in front of me.

I couldn't eat this!

"And where are you from?" asked another girl in a brittle voice. Her blonde hair was dyed in pink streaks and tied in a bun, her eyes were heavily made up, and she had silver pendant earrings.

"Guildford," I said.

"Never heard of it," she said dismissively. "Fran, how come she hasn't got a veggie burger like we've got?"

"Because this is Suzy's first meal, that's why," said Fran. "Rihanna, focus on eating, please; there's time to ask Suzy questions afterwards."

I ate one forkful of baked beans, then another. Tears came into my eyes, and I bit my lip. I noticed that Fran had sat down opposite me, and she said, "Suzy, put a piece of potato onto your fork and put it in your mouth."

I nearly gagged before I swallowed the potato. I took a long sip of my water.

"Good girl. Try to relax your shoulders," said Fran, as she removed my glass.

Nobody was speaking, and there was just the scraping of knives and forks. Suddenly I couldn't stand it any longer. I got up, holding my plate, and walked over to the bin I'd seen earlier. I pressed the foot-pedal and scraped everything in. Even the sound of people eating stopped. I held my breath, listened and waited.

Then I heard footsteps as someone marched over. "Suzy, I'm disappointed at your lack of trying," said Fran.

"I don't want it," I cried.

"You have to eat it," said Fran firmly. Already she was spooning more waffles and baked beans onto another plate, and putting it into the microwave. I walked back to the table and sat down. There was a loud ping and Fran handed me a warm plate. "Please try and eat it," she said.

I didn't dare meet anyone's eyes as I returned to my seat.

I sliced the potato angrily, and ate it mechanically. *I hated it here!*

"That's right, Suzy", said Fran, her eyes locked on my plate.

The time was nearly up. In just ten minutes I could leave the lounge and go upstairs to my horrible new pink room to cry. It was really quiet, as everyone was glued to *EastEnders*, waiting for the cliffhanger. These made-up relationships and teenage pregnancy that were just part of some plot really didn't touch me. Real life seemed far worse now that I was sitting on some sofa, miles from my friends and family who had abandoned me. Near the flat-screen telly, the girl with blonde hair tied in a bun was annoying me with her weird exercises, mostly done *en pointe*. Holding onto the windowsill like it was some bar, she stretched her leg so it nearly touched her chin. I'd noticed that the others had twice asked her to stop stretching.

The *EastEnders* closing music started then. Wyatt

said, "Hey, Suzy, sorry to have ignored you. It's just that we're addicted to the drama."

Rihanna now spoke, "That was really funny what you did at dinner."

"Yeah, Penny looked sooooo surprised," said Yun, who was drawing.

"Hey, Yun, let's see that," said Rihanna sharply.

"I dunno," she said, looking unsure.

"Go on, Yun, we want to see it," said Wyatt. "Don't we, Suzy?"

I smiled weakly. I could only think of all that food I'd eaten and the bloated feeling it had left in me.

Yun held up her drawing. I was surprised by how good the likeness was, showing Fran's angry face, like a giant cheese, hovering over the bin. Everyone was laughing.

Yun said, "I remember my first dinner here. I found it terrible. You've done well to get through it."

"But don't chuck food away again. Or we'll get pissed off," Rihanna said.

"You get pissed off with me," said the girl who was exercising.

"Leah, that's because you often take ages over dinner," said Wyatt, and he sighed. He turned to me, and said, "See, Penny doesn't normally let us leave the table until everyone's finished eating their food."

I noticed that the clock on the wall said eight. I had stayed for longer than thirty minutes in the lounge, which was the rule here. "I'm going upstairs to unpack. Goodnight," I said.

The others said "Goodnight," almost in a chorus.

I felt relieved to be out of there, although when I reached the landing, I got confused about the right direction to take. No, it was a different door which led to the staircase. Finally I reached the landing and went through the second door on the left. The bright pink walls seemed to close in on me, and the eaves strangely reminded me of my bedroom at home. I saw Yun's bed over in the corner. I felt disappointed that I didn't have my own room. At the bottom of my bed were my suitcases, and I tugged at the zip on one of them.

I fished inside for my things. There were leggings, baggy T-shirts and woolly jumpers from my Fat Days, a teddy bear that I'd forgotten about, a wash-bag; but only practical things like my electric toothbrush and soap, and no make-up or perfume. Mum hadn't packed any of the stuff I actually wanted. She was trying to treat me like a little kid while I was locked up in here, all of my rights and freedom stripped away.

I buried my head in my pillow and started to cry.

"PLEASE DON'T TUBE ME"

"Cheer up," Wyatt said. "It's not that bad here."

"Yes, it is," I answered. No food diary with me, I'd been writing down everything I'd eaten that day in a notebook. I pushed it under the cushion, so that Wyatt couldn't see.

"No, seriously," he said. "This place is okay. But do you mind if I give you some advice?"

"What's that?"

"Stay on the right side of Penny, or she can be a bitch," Wyatt said. He frowned, poking his fingers through the hole in the sleeve of his red jumper.

"In what way?"

"After Penny caught me exercising in my room, staff wouldn't leave me on my own for a week. Stupid, I know, to get caught," and he sighed. "I wasn't allowed to do any exercise until I'd gained two kilos. It was a bit harsh, wasn't it?" But he still smiled.

I stared at him. I'd have exercised anyway.

He went on, "But Penny's okay, if you don't break the rules."

"Well, it doesn't matter to me," I said. "Coz I

won't be staying much longer."

"Why's that?" Wyatt asked. He was looking really curious.

"Mum's going to come back for me," I said, trying to sound as confident as I could. "When she feels guilty enough about leaving me here, she'll realise she's made a big mistake. Right?"

Wyatt gave a wry smile. "I don't want to disappoint you, but most people think that when they get here. And everyone ends up staying until they reach their target weight. So there's little point in hoping that your mum will change her mind."

I stared miserably back at him.

"C'mon," he said. "Us lot aren't that bad, and it's actually quite fun here sometimes."

"Sorry, it's just it's a real shock."

"You'll get used to it." He punched me playfully on the arm as he went out.

No, I'll never get used to it, I wanted to shout. *Anyway, he didn't know my mum. She'd change her mind, probably.*

Someone was shouting my name. I remembered with horror where I was. I pulled the duvet over my head, hoping they would go away. I wanted to go back into my dream...*I'd been cantering down a hill, and my horse had just got ahead of Nick's horse...*

"I've called your name twice, and you haven't answered." It was Penny's voice. "Why haven't you got up already...humm? You know that breakfast is served sharp at eight. Everyone else is already eating. And you're still lying in bed. Will you get up!"

"I don't want any." I wished she would just go

away. What right had she to boss me around anyway? But Penny was wresting the duvet off me.

I hugged myself, feeling very exposed.

"It's not a choice," Penny said angrily. "Everyone eats each meal. I thought you understood that."

"Well, I'm not the others," I shouted. "And I don't want breakfast!"

"Here's the choice," Penny said in a firm voice, "Either you're downstairs for breakfast in ten minutes, or you'll be taken down there in your nightdress to eat it. Do you want that?"

I started to panic. I was wearing my horrible nightie with a bear on the front chewing a red rose. No way did I want the others seeing it. "No, I'm getting up," I said.

"You've got ten minutes, or I mean what I've said."

"Nut cluster or strawberry crunch?" Penny asked.

I stared at the silver topped bottles of milk. Full fat.

"Well, if you can't make up your mind, nut cluster it is." She seemed to pour torrents of milk into the bowl. "Here."

I took the bowl, and mumbled, "Thanks." I walked numbly round to the empty place at the table. "I can't have full-fat milk," I said. "It's not healthy, my grandpa isn't allowed full-fat. It could make his blood clot and cause a heart attack."

"That's nonsense in your case," said Penny. "You're a very underweight girl. And you need full-fat milk. Calcium is important for your bones, and the fat in the milk cushions your organs and helps your reproductive system."

"Suzy, can you sit down," Fran said. "It distracts the others from eating their breakfasts, you getting upset. The thing is to put some cereal onto your spoon and eat it in two bites. Can you do that now, please?"

I pushed a spoonful into my mouth and nearly gagged.

"And another spoon," Fran said. "If you don't think about it first, it's easier."

"Leah, don't push your cereal round your bowl," said Penny. "Come on, let's have you all eating normally."

I started building banks in my bowl, so in the middle I had a pool, where I swirled the milk round.

"You can all get down, except for Suzy," said Penny.

I watched as the others went out.

Penny was sitting next to Fran and they were both facing me. I felt outnumbered. Penny said, "I'm fed up with your games, young lady. This can't go on, can it, Fran?"

Fran shook her head.

"What do you mean?" I asked nervously.

Penny went on: "Wednesday night, you threw away the waffles; yesterday, you messed around with the portions I gave you; and now you're refusing to eat breakfast." There was a long pause, and then she said, "If you won't eat this, I'll have to tube-feed you, because if you lose more weight there is a risk that you will die."

"But I can refuse to be tube-fed," I said.

"No, you can't," said Penny. "We sedate you, then tube-feed you. You don't have any choice."

"So it's best to eat this," said Fran.

There was a noise and the door opened. A tall, broad-shouldered man stood in the doorway. He wore a grey suit, a cream shirt, a bright Rupert Bear tie. I wondered if he was another nurse come to hold me down if I refused to eat.

"So, what have you decided?" asked Penny.

"I'll eat it," I said reluctantly. I pushed a spoonful of cereal into my mouth. *I'd no choice left!*

Yun was drawing a brilliant portrait of Wyatt's head and shoulders, with random squiggly letters from the alphabet positioned to make the hairline and shirt. The tutor came back across the room from the computers. You couldn't go on the internet, so I wasn't able to message Nick or Molly.

Mike was the man I'd seen in the kitchen earlier. "It's very quiet over here. I'm glad to see you're all working hard," he said.

I hadn't realised that the others would be so bright when I'd been left at the clinic, but it was obvious that my achievements didn't make me stand out here.

"Mike, does that tie sing?" Rihanna asked.

"Yes. Do you want to hear it?" He sounded pleased that she'd asked. He pushed the bear's bowtie. The bear's eyes lit up red, and the tie moved up and down jerkily, as a man sang 'Happy Birthday'.

Rihanna said, "But it's not anyone's birthday, is it?"

"No, but you could imagine it is," Mike said, and smiled.

The door opened and a tall girl with short, curly black hair stepped into the room with the long, quick steps of someone who was confident. She pushed her phone into her pocket, and looked round at us. She had to be in her late teens.

"What are you back for, Zoe?" asked Wyatt.

"I've lost four kilos," she said. "So I've got to stay over the weekend to put it back on."

"A weekend binge, right?" Wyatt said, and grinned.

"Something like that," she said, pulling a face. "It sucks being back. Sorry, it's nice to see everyone again, but I've got to eat 4,000 calories a day." She let out a big sigh. "Anorexics don't even eat that on the wards."

I stared at her, horrified. I hadn't known that you got re-admitted if you lost weight.

"How's Uni going?" Mike asked her.

"Pretty good," she said, and smiled. "Though we medical students get loads more work than everyone else."

She must be training to be a doctor and I tried hard to hide my surprise. Mike walked over to the computers again, hopefully out of earshot. I cleared my throat nervously, and said in a low voice, "Zoe? Sorry, we've not met before. But do you mind telling me if it's lawful for a doctor to threaten to tube-feed someone?"

Zoe looked surprised, and then a smile appeared on her face. "Is that what Penny has said she'd do?" she asked.

"Yeah, this morning at breakfast."

Zoe looked unsurprised, and said, "She said that to me too, when I first came here."

"Zoe, didn't she tube you?" asked Wyatt.

"Well, yes," Zoe said, and laughed. I thought that she looked embarrassed. She went on, "It happened after a few days here. I'd decided that Penny wasn't really serious about tubing me, so I refused lunch. And the next thing I knew, I was being given a sedative; though it still took three staff to hold me down when Penny put the tube in, and through it they fed me a high-calorie feed liquid."

"Quite a bit of manpower needed then," said Wyatt.

Some of the others laughed. Horrified, I stared at Zoe.

"Penny says it to pretty much everyone here," Yun told me. "I'd just eat if I were you."

I stared down at my book, completely gutted.

I'd gone up to my room to get a jumper. I stared at the pile of my things on the floor. *Who had moved them?*

Yun entered the room, and she held a long purple towel round her. Another towel was wrapped tightly round her head. "Hi," she said.

I was so wound up, I felt I couldn't ignore the fact that my things had been moved. "Was there something wrong with my stuff being on the dresser?" I asked.

She looked surprised. "Oh, I didn't think you'd mind if I moved them," she said. "I really wanted to keep those bottom two shelves of the dresser. You can put your things anywhere else. There's an empty cupboard over there." She pointed to the door beside my bed.

I hadn't even looked in there, so I couldn't really say anything.

"You're lucky you arrived yesterday, coz you've missed fish and chips," Yun said, pulling a face. "It's delivered from the local fish shop, and the fish is fried in batter. It's absolutely gross!"

"When's that meal?"

"Wednesday lunchtime," she said. "That was why I was so happy my school show was that day." She disappeared behind the screen, and threw her towel over the top of it.

She was so confident, I felt intimidated. What was sharing going to be like? For already she'd divided up the space, and she was the one who wanted things staying how they were, my stuff fitting round hers.

She said, "What does this look like?"

She came out wearing a denim dress that was way too small, but I needed to pick my words carefully. "Well, it's a bit ..."

"Tight," Yun said, finishing my sentence. "I forget how much weight I've put on. It used to be my favourite dress."

I felt bad now, but she'd already disappeared behind the screen again. *Would I look like that in a few weeks' time?* It was really scary to think that.

"Does this look better?" she asked.

It was leggings and a purple tunic top that she wore now.

"Yeah. That's really nice."

"We're actually only meant to wear baggy things in here, so we don't think so much about the weight we're gaining. I always forget," said Yun, and laughed.

That must be why Mum had packed my Fat

Clothes!

I came into the kitchen to hear the liquidiser whining. Fran then poured a strawberry milkshake into two glasses and handed them to Zoe and Leah, who both looked miserable.

Fran turned round to the others and said, "Girls, you need to stay together in Woodstock. Do you all know what time you need to be back?"

"Yeah, six," said Rihanna, and pulled a face. "We won't miss this place."

"I don't expect you to. It's not here for that," said Fran, and smiled.

I watched them as Rihanna and Yun left. Rihanna grinned over at Zoe and me, and stuck her finger up behind Fran's back, before closing the door.

Fran turned to Leah, who was staring at the milkshake, though Zoe was halfway through hers. "Leah, can you suck the milkshake up properly through the straw," Fran said sharply, "or you'll need to drink it straight from the glass."

I saw Leah glare at Fran. She seemed to have a temper on her, and I didn't want to wait for the explosion. I went through to the lounge and out of the patio doors. Outside there was a brilliant blue sky, and I slumped down onto a bench. It felt hard and uncomfortable.

I missed Nick. And I couldn't even Facebook him. I started to cry. I didn't stop when I heard someone coming, in fact I cried more loudly. I wanted people to know how much I hated it here. Fran sat down on the bench and put her arm round me.

"The first few days can feel really difficult, until you've settled in," Fran said in her soft voice, passing me some tissues. "You must be missing your family and friends. Your mum phoned again this morning to ask how you are. Would you like to talk to her?"

I shook my head, and said, "I don't care about her."

"You're angry with her, aren't you?"

I nodded.

"I know she cares a great deal about you," said Fran. "She wants you to get better. She believes the best way to help is for you to be here with us."

"But now I'm going to miss out on going to Switzerland with my orchestra."

"When's the trip?" asked Fran.

"In December," I said.

"I don't see any reason why you can't go, if the trip's in December. That's if you cooperate with us, because in three months you should be at your target weight, and feeling healthy again."

I forced a smile. I just couldn't get my mind round my new target weight, which was a BMI of 20.

Fran was looking thoughtful, and said, "In the meantime, why don't I ask your mum to bring your cello here? Music would give you something else to think about, other than food, wouldn't it?" She smiled, "Maybe you can write a list of other things you want here as well?"

"Okay," I said. But if my stuff was brought here, then maybe I was staying.

The others each lifted their right knee and were reaching their left hand up into the air. The dance music was really blasting from the stereo in the corner.

"They're so lucky," Leah told me. "Penny won't let me exercise, coz I had my dance class this morning."

"I used to go running twice a day." I went on, "Now, I'm just expected to sit around, stuffing myself."

"I can't wait for Exeat weekend," said Leah. "My sister's getting us passes for a spa."

"To do what?"

She didn't answer. She glanced across at the others, and her face looked worried. I guessed there must be a gym or exercise class at the spa.

"Look, Suzy," Leah said quickly. "Don't tell anyone about the spa. It's only something my sister mentioned. We mightn't even go there, as it's ages away. I'll be such a beached whale by then, probably I won't want anyone to see me in my gym stuff." She managed to laugh, but I could tell she was worried.

"No, you won't be," I said. But my words sounded hollow, and my face felt hot.

"Well, won't you feel like that when you reach your target weight?"

There was no good way out of this one. I risked a glance at her, and said, "Yeah, I guess so."

"So? See what I'm saying."

"All right. But at least you'll be out of here."

"I don't care much. I've been in loads of these places."

"Really?"

"Yes. Three hospitals, including this one," she said.

I tried to work out how many months this added up to. The total must be over six months. Nobody could seriously believe this was okay, with the loss of freedom and everything. It made me feel churned up inside to think about it.

Leah went on, "And it's a waste of time. The nurses and doctors think they can brainwash me into wanting to eat, but they can't."

The door opened, and it was Yun. I was glad of the interruption. She said, "Suzy, your mum's in the kitchen talking to Penny. I thought you'd want to know."

"Yes, thanks," I said. Suddenly I felt sick. "Did you hear what they're saying?"

"No, sorry," Yun said, and smiled. "You'd best go and find out."

I went down the corridor into the kitchen. No one was there, but I saw my metallic turquoise cello case propped up against a chair, and some big blue bags that I recognised from home, piled onto the table.

There were voices speaking in the hallway.

"...I couldn't believe it when I found the diary the girl in Suzy's class gave her." It was Mum talking. "That Gemma's really got something to answer for."

"It's a shame," said Penny. "Often we find girls here have been bullied." Penny came through to the kitchen followed by Mum.

Mum had a surprised look on her face. "Hello, darling," she said. "How are you feeling?"

"Mum, what were you saying about my diary? I want it back, it's mine," I said. My voice sounded breathless, I was so tense. Suddenly it occurred to me that she must have searched my room to find it. "You've gone through my stuff, haven't you? My bedroom's private!"

"No, I haven't," said Mum. "I needed to find the

things you've asked me to bring."

I recalled the list that I'd written for Fran.

Mum turned round to Penny, and said, "You think I shouldn't be giving Suzy the diary at the moment?"

"No, keep hold of it," said Penny.

"I hate you!" I shouted at Mum. I grabbed the nearest bag from the table and stormed through to the lounge.

Before the fire door shut, I heard Penny say to Mum, "I'm afraid that anorexia can temporarily change their personalities. A loving child can become angry and say hurtful, unkind things they would never normally say ..."

The door closed. Putting the heavy bag down, I slumped against the wall. *What did Penny know? It wasn't as if she lived inside my head and knew what it felt like to have my diary stolen!*

THE LETTER

Leah sat on the lounge carpet looking at the telly, sobbing as she watched herself dancing. I almost wanted to slip out again unnoticed, but just then she turned round. Her mascara had run, creating panda streaks down her cheeks, but she didn't seem to care.

I sat down beside her and put my arm round her. "What's the matter?" I asked.

"I'll never dance like that again. I've forgotten my technique...and now I've got fat."

"No, you're not fat," I said quickly. But I knew the pressure on dancers to be thin. "What's the ballet you were in?"

"The Nutcracker. It was a professional production. I was the butterfly."

"I know what you mean about technique," I said. "I feel the same way about my cello. I've hardly done any practice since I got here."

Leah's face brightened up: "I didn't know you played the cello. Can you play Bach? Will you play, if I dance?"

"Sure. When do you want to?"

"What about now?" she said, smiling.

Prelude to Bach's First Suite. Leah was dancing and I was playing my cello. It was almost like we'd rehearsed this before, it moved so well. We had an audience of the others, but no one was even chatting any more.

Leah's steps were so graceful, as she twirled around, but I had to concentrate on my bowing. *Enjoy it, Julia always said.* I missed Julia, I thought as I bit my lip. I added some vibrato to the notes so they really sang.

"That was beautiful, girls," Fran said at the end. "I loved the way the cello and dancing went together."

I hadn't noticed her come in, and I was surprised to see her looking quite tearful.

I'd found her and Penny searching my room, all my things out on my bed. I felt the rage building up inside me.

"Again," said Yun.

Fran said, "Well, there's time for another piece before dinner."

I struggled to think of something to play and looked across at Leah who had her leg stretched up to her chin, a position that looked really painful to me. Then, Paganini's 'Witches' Dance' came into my mind. I grinned and started to play.

I looked up and saw Leah *en pointe*, pointing her leg forwards and backwards, quite robotically. I caught her eye, and she smiled at me. Good. She knew that this piece was meant to take the piss. The others were laughing.

"Thanks for that. Best you put your cello away safely upstairs," Fran said.

If I'd been with Julia, I could have played on and on. To my annoyance, my eyes were filling with tears. I pushed my cello into its case, struggling with the locks.

"I'll take it from you," said Fran.

I wasn't even allowed to lift the cello up the stairs, even though I'd always carried it everywhere. Fran had said lifting it was too much strain for me. I watched as she carried it by the handle in a way that I wouldn't, but I didn't say anything.

The others had gone through to the kitchen, stupidly eager to be on time. I went through. Vaguely, I saw the yoghurts on the counter and noticed that the others had scrawled initials on them in black pen. There should be two empty seats at the table, because Zoe had been discharged that afternoon. But there was only one available seat that was directly under Penny's hawk-eyes. Sitting down, I saw that it was the toffee flavour yoghurt that was left. No one had wanted it yesterday because it had the highest number of calories in it.

"Suzy, could you start your pizza?" Penny asked.

"Why've I been left with the toffee yoghurt?" I said. "It's not fair."

Nobody said anything; there was just the scraping of the others' knives and forks as they ate.

"If you'd been here earlier, you could have chosen yours," Penny said. She smiled at me in that sarcastic way of hers. "For such a talented girl, the fact you continue to be so preoccupied with ways to avoid eating a few extra calories is surprising."

"Everyone else is doing the same," I muttered.

"Shut up, we don't," snapped Rihanna.

I felt so angry with everyone; still I surprised myself when I blurted out, "You're all a bunch of freaks. I mean who else eats in silence. It's not exactly normal. Your friends must stare at you when you eat out. But probably you don't have any friends."

"That's not nice. And it's not true," said Penny.

"Speak for yourself," shouted Rihanna, who sat opposite me. "We're not the ones dressed like a saddo."

I looked down at the horrible flowery shirt I was wearing.

"Yeah, shut up!" shouted Yun.

"Yes." Rihanna shouted, "You're always going on and on about feeling fat after meals, when the rest of us are trying to forget the bloated feeling."

"I don't go on like you, Suzy, do I?" said Leah.

No one said anything. Then, I mumbled, "I don't care what people think here."

"You should do," said Penny, looking at my face closely. "Suzy, you want to have friends here, don't you? At the moment you're alienating everyone."

Tears welled up in my eyes as I forced another bit of pizza into my mouth. It had grown cold and greasy.

"You'd better take off that bracelet. She won't weigh you with it on," said Yun.

I stared down at my silver bracelet, made from chunky links that were joined together. *It weighed hardly anything, nothing to make a fuss about.*

At least Yun was talking to me. Everyone had pretty much ignored me since dinner last night. Leah appeared in the corridor, red-eyed and sniffing loudly. Yun put her arm round Leah, and said, "Didn't you gain?"

"Nah, I've lost," she said, sounding bitter. "Now I can't go out at the weekend with my family."

"Blame Penny," said Wyatt. "She hasn't been putting enough butter on the potatoes.

The others laughed, and Leah even smiled.

"Suzy!"

I hadn't expected for Penny to call me next. Just thinking about how much weight I'd gained made me feel faint.

"You'd better go in," Wyatt said. "Good luck!"

Penny was writing on her clipboard as I entered, and she looked up briefly. She said, "Same drill as last time. Take your clothes off, leaving just your underwear on."

I didn't want to undress, but I had little choice.

"Right, onto the scales. Let's see what your weight is," said Penny. "Don't worry, most of the increase will be your body rehydrating with fluid."

What if it wasn't?

Her brown eyes were carefully reading the counter. "You've gained 2.5 kilos," she said slowly. "The good news is that you can start activities today...well, so long as it's not high-impact things like aerobics."

"I can't believe I've gained so much," I blurted. I was losing control over the one thing I cared about.

"Don't get upset," she said. "Everyone gains more in the first week. Most of it is water." She smiled at me. "You can put on your clothes now. Then call Yun in."

I was glad to get off the scales. I didn't believe her about the water.

"It's exciting for us when someone gets letters," Wyatt said at breakfast. He was looking at the pile Penny had just given me, after I'd finished the cereal and the crumpet.

I decided that she must have been saving them up.

"You must be really popular, getting all these," said Yun, and she smiled across at me.

"Yeah," said Leah. She glanced at the letter I held in my hand. "Who's that letter from?"

It surprised me that the others were nicer now. I said, "Oh, my granny, I think." I hadn't heard anything from my grandparents since I'd been brought here. My fingers trembled, ripping open the envelope. My eyes skimmed down the page of Granny's large, loopy writing, stopping at this sentence: "Now you're eating three good meals a day, you soon won't know yourself..." How could she write that? Like eating lots of food here was the answer, when all I wanted was to be skinny.

"If we could receive emails, we could keep up with our friends more," said Rihanna.

Penny pounced on this. "Well, you can receive letters."

"That's embarrassing," said Rihanna sulkily. "I don't want everyone knowing I'm here."

The staff didn't trust us with sending emails, or using the internet. They treated us like little kids here!

Becky was looking over my shoulder. "Who's that letter from? The turquoise pen's really cool."

"It's from my boyfriend," I said, recognising Nick's handwriting straightaway. Pulling out his letter, he'd drawn a column of turquoise hearts on both sides of the page. He couldn't have dumped me, like I'd feared.

"Oh cool," said Yun, and she smiled. "I wish I had a boyfriend!"

"Yeah, you're really lucky," said Leah.

"Aren't you opening that one?" asked Yun, pushing a letter towards me.

"It's from my mum," I said. But I could see Penny looking across at me, so I added, "Yeah, I guess I'd better open it."

My heart skipped a few beats. That was Gemma's writing inside. How had she got my address here? I mustn't let anyone read the letter.

Luckily Penny said something just then and I managed to slip the letter into my pocket, unnoticed. "OK, time to hear today's activities," she said. "This afternoon it's the art therapy group, and for those who know who they are, there's ice-skating."

And that meant other people, of course. I wasn't allowed to exercise yet.

Flicking through the biology textbook, I found a picture of an experiment where a burning peanut is heating the little cylinder of water above it. Was that how much energy a peanut gave off? Imagine eating a whole Snickers Bar that was stuffed full of peanuts; this was what some of the others, who were on extra calories, had to do at break. I wondered how many times I'd have to run round the school racetrack to burn off one Snickers Bar.

"Eleven," said Mike, glancing at his watch. "Those of you who need refreshments, can you go to the kitchen, please."

"Suzy," Yun said, "are you coming to the lounge with us?"

I remembered the letter in my pocket from Gemma. "No, it's okay. But thanks," I said, and smiled.

"Suzy, it's important to take regular breaks," Mike said. "You've been working very hard."

I'd got the impression that he'd decided I was a workaholic. It was like you couldn't do anything here to excess without it being labelled as a problem or an obsession. "No, I just want to read my magazine," I said.

I saw Mike look over at the magazine, then at the computers, checking that I couldn't get onto any of them, as the password box was still displayed on each screen. "Well, see you shortly," he said.

I waited until they were all definitely gone, and then pulled out the letter. It was warm and crumpled. I needed to read it twice, because the first time I couldn't take the words in.

I've heard from Ben that you've gone into a clinic to receive treatment for anorexia. I hope that it's a nice place, and you settle in quickly, and that the doctors are able to help you.

I'm really scared, because yesterday morning in break Ben pushed me up against a wall, and he and Nick were shouting at me that I'm to blame for you getting ill. I thought that Ben was going to hit me, and now I'm frightened to go into school. He's really angry with me because your mum's found the food diary I gave you ages ago, with the dieting tips in it. Remember, you asked me for help with losing weight, and I was happy to help a year ago when you were getting teased. I thought that if you lost a few kilos you'd be more confident and happier. I never expected the diet to go this far, and last term, I asked you if you were still dieting because I was worried about how thin you were getting, and you told me that you weren't.

I really don't want to get bullied by the others for something that's not my fault. If you agree with what I've said, please can you write to Nick or Ben, or send a letter via your mum telling them this.

Thanks.

Love Gemma

I ripped the letter into tiny pieces, sprinkling them into the bin like they were confetti.

"I think a walk's a good idea," said Penny, laughing. "It might blow a few cobwebs away."

I stared at her, in shock. No freedom for so many days that it felt unreal to be able to leave the clinic's grounds.

"You'll need a coat, it's cold out," said Fran.

Yun and the others were standing near the door, ready to go out. "I'll just be a minute," I blurted, and sprinted upstairs to my room. It was a relief when I got downstairs and saw that the others were still there.

"All right?" Wyatt asked.

I nodded and grinned. But I waited until I was out of earshot of the ward's kitchen window before I punched the air, and shouted, "I'm finally free!"

"It can feel like that," Yun said. "When you've been stuck here for a few days."

I felt quite choked looking up at the leaves. In just a few days, they'd changed colour to burnt gold and fiery reds.

Wyatt held the gate open for me, and said, "Don't start doing a runner on us now. We'd never forgive you. And it always takes a hell of a lot of explaining when you come back without someone."

We were passing the first sandy-coloured house, called The Old Bakehouse, which I was told was where Penny lived with her family. The pink roses made it look homely. It was weird, when she was so scary, to think that she had two teenage sons, a husband and two tortoiseshell cats. The cats we'd met a few times when they'd jumped over the fence into the clinic's garden.

After a while, Wyatt and Rihanna stopped and turned towards us.

Rihanna went on, "We want to sneak into Blenheim for a run – don't grass on us though."

I was surprised by how serious she looked.

"Don't worry, I'm not a grass," I said, my stomach now churning.

We took a sharp left, and ended up at the top of a steep hill with just a path leading down, broken by widely spaced steps. The others had started to run down it.

I followed after them, wishing that I wasn't wearing ballet pumps. I was glad to catch up with

Rihanna and Wyatt.

"Did you see the sign?" Wyatt asked me.

"No, where?" I asked, breathlessly.

"At the top. This is called Hoggrove Hill. We're the hogs Penny's fattening up to roast on her spit," he said, and grinned.

"Don't, Wy," said Yun. "Suzy probably doesn't want to hear that."

"What? She won't have nightmares," said Wyatt. "Oh, c'mon, it's funny."

I saw that Yun's face had relaxed into a smile. "Okay...but still it's a bit raw thinking of it," she said.

"Then roast it longer," said Wyatt, grinning.

"That's so naff," said Rihanna. "Wait. Stop!"

"What is it?" Wyatt asked.

"Leah's waving," said Rihanna. Leah had turned round and was staring at a silver car rushing past us. "That was Bird Cage!" she called out.

I knew that this was what the others called Dr Avery.

"D'you reckon she saw us?" I asked Wyatt.

"Dunno," said Wyatt. "If she did, she'll know where we're going. And we'll be in trouble."

"WHY D'YOU THINK WE'RE HERE UNLESS WE COULD DIE?"

I started the afternoon writing in my diary in the garden, but once I came in the time started to drag. There was a film about vampires on in the lounge, but no one was watching it. I went into the kitchen to find everyone gathered there, even though it wasn't time for dinner.

"Suzy?" said Penny, in a welcoming voice.

She was wearing a loose green dress, and she'd just had her hair done so it looked softer and quite pretty. Luckily, no mention was made of the run the day before. It was as if Bird Cage hadn't caught us.

Penny said, "I've just told the others that a documentary's going to be made here. The television company are interested in filming the re-feeding programme we offer on the ward and the therapeutic activities that you do here." She looked directly at me. "They're keen to ask each of you about what it's like having an eating disorder as a young person." Her brown eyes studied my face. "Are you interested in being in it?"

"I dunno," I said. "When will the filming start?"

"Soon," she said. "Maybe in a week or so. The others want to be in the film, but there's no pressure for you to. It's your decision, but it could help people who've not had access to the kind of help you've had."

I felt I couldn't really say no. "I'll be in it too," I said.

"I'll have to get permission from your parents as you're under sixteen, but thanks for your interest. That's helpful." She glanced at her watch, and said, "Suzy, you have therapy starting with Joe shortly."

Therapy! Only crazy people saw psychologists. "I don't need to see a psychologist. I'm not mad!" I blurted out.

"I didn't say that, did I?" said Penny. "A psychologist helps you to understand the issues that may have caused you to develop a problem with food."

"But I don't want to see one." It was awful having no choice over what I ate, but talking about private stuff with some stranger, that was nearly as bad.

"Therapy isn't negotiable," said Penny. "It's not a holiday camp here, is it?" She gave the others a wry smile. They responded nervously. "Young people are here to get better. Come on, Suzy."

We went down a long corridor, Penny leading the way. "Joe's in the room on the right. Good luck!"

I was surprised by the look of this young man: in his twenties, with hair a bit like the drummer in a band I liked, standing beside a desk, holding a file. *What had he been reading about me?*

"You must be Suzy. I'm Joe. Come in," he said,

with a welcoming smile.

I sat down in the leather chair.

"So why do you think you're here?" he asked.

"Dunno," I said sulkily. "Coz I've been told to come here."

"That may be," he said, still smiling. "Here we only talk about things you want to. It's your space."

"Meaning I talk, you listen?"

"Yes, but I'll say things as well. And we'll explore together any concerns or difficulties you may have, and other things you want to talk about. Is that okay?"

"I guess so," I said reluctantly. I started to play with the loose strands of the blue tassel on my skirt. It was somehow comforting having something to fiddle with.

"So, how are you settling in?"

"Okay, the others are nice...but the meals are horrible. We never stop eating. It can't be good for me, having my tummy swelling up all the time."

"I'm afraid I can't change the menu, that's the dietician's area," he said. "But we can talk about what eating the food feels like. You sound very distressed by this."

"Yes. Well, I'm used to eating far less," I said.

"What did you eat before you came here?"

"Just melon, apples, low-fat yoghurt, and I drank loads of Diet Coke," I said. "But I needed to be on a diet. I was fat before."

"Do you think you restrict the food you eat too much?"

"No...I'm not anorexic," I said. "My diet just got out of control."

"I don't think a label like anorexia's helpful. It's

about understanding what you're experiencing," said Joe. "That's an interesting expression you've used, *getting out-of-control.* Is that what your diet felt like?"

"Maybe a bit," I said. But then I clammed up, feeling I'd given away too much.

Joe looked down at his file. "So, you live at home with your mum and stepdad Rupert...and you've got a brother?"

"Yes."

"And how do you get on with them?"

"All right," I said. "I'm close to Ben, my brother. He's just two years older than me."

"And what about your dad?"

"I haven't seen him since I was two, when my parents divorced."

"That's very sad," said Joe, and he looked genuinely sorry about it. "Does your mum have contact with him?"

"No. She doesn't know where he is," I said, finding it hard to get the words out. "She's really angry about it too, coz my dad doesn't pay her any money to help with the bills."

"Would you like to see your dad?" Joe asked.

I stared at him. No one had ever asked me that question. At home it was like my dad hadn't existed. I'd only found out his name - Nigel - by eavesdropping on one of Mum's conversations when I was little. And it was really difficult to tell what someone was like from two photos. "I dunno if I want to meet him," I said slowly.

"Well, it's something you might think about," said Joe, as if it might in fact be a possibility. I began to warm to him slightly. There was a long pause, then he said, "And what do you do in your free time, Suzy?"

"I play the cello."

"The cello's a favourite instrument of mine," he said. "I play the guitar."

Again, I began to feel impressed.

"How long have you played?" he asked.

"Since I was eight. I've won lots of competitions too," I said. But I then worried that this sounded boastful, so I added, "But I flunked the Young Soloists' Competition in the summer. I didn't get past the first round."

"What happened?"

"My pieces just didn't sound good. I kind of lost my nerve."

"And how does it feel when you don't win something?"

"Awful. I feel I've let Mum and Julia down. Julia's my cello teacher," I said quickly. "So, I just practise harder." I turned my eyes down to the bright rug on the floor.

"That sounds like a lot of pressure," he said.

"Not really," I said. "Everyone in my family wins things. My cousin Sarah's studying maths at Oxford University, and her brother Jonathan's applying there too."

"So you feel you need to keep up with them?" Joe asked, trying to lead me on.

"Well, I guess so," I said. "I'm not much good at maths though...music's my thing."

"It sounds like it's not just your mum and your teacher putting pressure on you; you're also the one doing it," said Joe, looking thoughtful. "This is something we can return to."

He looked at his watch. "We'd better leave it there today. We'll meet at the same time next week. Is that okay?"

"Okay," I said, but even though he'd been nice, I wasn't at all sure about going back next week.

We'd just got into Oxford's University Parks, and rain was spitting down. It was Sunday and my first visit out, so this didn't seem fair. I felt quite mixed up, because Mum had given me a lovely silver scarf from Julia. It showed that she was thinking about me, and that she cared.

"Let's hope it stops," said Mum.

"The heavens aren't allowed to open, are they?" said Granny. "Your grandfather needs to have a word with Him upstairs."

I knew that Grandpa was a non-believer like me. "There isn't anything upstairs," I muttered.

"If you were open to the possibility, then you might not be in this pickle now," said Granny.

"Why don't I get us all an ice cream?" suggested Rupert, tactfully changing the subject. "Suzy, we'll tell Penny you've eaten one, then she can deduct the calories from your daily amount."

I could tell that he was trying hard to see things through my eyes. But I wasn't about to eat anything. Anyway, usually you had to get Penny's agreement first for this; otherwise, she didn't count the calories. "I just want a Diet Coke," I said.

"Go on, it's only one ice cream," Granny said.

"Mum, stop it!" Mum said sharply to her.

I was surprised that Mum had stuck up for me, as if she understood my struggle with calories.

"Good idea," Ben said to me. "Have a sneaky Diet Coke while you can."

He knew I wasn't allowed fizzy drinks in the clinic, because I'd moaned about this on the way here. "It's only one can," I said, shrugging my shoulders.

"Yeah," Ben said. "But don't you get a ban on watching telly, or something, if you get caught drinking the stuff?"

"No," I said, laughing.

Rupert handed me my Diet Coke. It was raining hard now, and I felt a drop roll down my cheek.

"We'd best go into that museum round the corner. Or, you'll catch cold, lass," said Grandpa. "Is the museum okay for you?"

I didn't mind Grandpa saying this, because I knew he was referring to the fact that I wasn't wearing warm clothes, and not that I was too thin.

The Pitt Rivers was crowded, with dinosaurs as well as people. Considering the size of the Iguandon, it was hard to believe it had been vegetarian. With its enormous bones in its head and ribcage, I tried to imagine it swishing its tail. Ben held up his mobile to take a photo – he'd put it on Facebook, probably. Curiously he didn't want me in the photo. Maybe he just didn't want to ask in case I got upset. I probably would do as well.

We moved on to the T-Rex. I turned to Mum as we passed the giant skeleton. I thought she might be more open to discussing my target weight, after what she'd said in the park about the ice cream. I said, "Mum, you know my target weight. Do you think

Penny might reduce it? It's just I really can't be 52 kilos again."

"You're not going on about weight again, Suzy," Mum said, and she sighed.

"But when I was that weight, people at school were still teasing me," I said miserably. I stared down at the blurb written about the T-Rex, unable to read it.

"Boys prefer girls with curves, don't they, Alec?" Granny said to Grandpa.

Grandpa nodded. "Aye. No man wants to put his arm round a sack of bones, lass," he said to me.

"Suzy, you don't want to be bony like the T-Rex, do you?" Ben said. "It's not exactly pretty. I don't think Nick would like you looking like that. He keeps asking after you, you know."

I quickly changed the subject away from Nick. "I'm never going to be massively tall, with a tail," I said sarcastically.

"Maybe not," said Ben, and grinned. "But still those girls on those pro-ana websites that Amber's told me about look gross."

I stared at him, panicking now that he knew about *litebitetara* and all the pro-ana sites I'd used. But I'd deleted the search history each time, even when using my own laptop. I said, "I didn't know you two had kept in touch."

"Yeah, we're together," said Ben. "And Mum's said that Amber can come over and stay with us in the Christmas holidays, haven't you, Mum?"

Mum turned back to us both. "Yes, if you're up to date with your coursework, Ben, and Amber's family are happy about it."

"They are," replied Ben.

I felt upset that I hadn't been consulted, even though I hadn't been there. I wasn't keen about seeing Amber again.

"Lass, they've got some old musical instruments here," said Grandpa, passing me a brochure. "Shall we go and have a look at the wee fiddles?"

"Suzy, your cello's probably old enough to be among them," said Rupert, smiling at me.

"Dunno about that," I said, shrugging my shoulders. I was annoyed about how hard he was trying.

I walked down the steps with Grandpa and Ben, and heard Mum say excitedly, "Suzy, I've found this fiddle that's shaped like a peacock. Look."

Everyone knew that peacocks were unlucky, and I sighed. I walked on to the next glass cabinet and paused in front of a clarinet. It was an E-flat clarinet: Molly's instrument, but a much older version made in 1915. I really missed Molly. In her last letter she'd said that orchestra rehearsals weren't much fun without me, but they weren't playing the better music until next term. Tears welled up in my eyes. I was desperate that life was carrying on without me.

I chewed on my pen, trying to think of what to write to Nick. He'd written to me several times, even sending me the love song he'd composed for me a few months ago, with a cute bear holding a red silk heart. Now he was really worried about how I'd gone quiet on him. Nick reckoned either I had to be dead and no one had told him, or I'd found a cute boy in the clinic who I liked more than him.

He couldn't be more wrong. But how did I start

to write what I had to say? I decided it needed a poem. I wrote:

THE END OF US?

You wrote a song about my smile;
Brimming compliments spilled into notes.
It felt a trial
To hear how seeing me could float
You high
And like romantic poets you'd sigh.
Blue china eyes, long wavy hair
You made me sound like a mermaid.
One who can dare
To wear anything. A spell made
By love
Binding us closely, our treasure trove.

But now my bloated tummy too gross
To even look at, you'll dump me
When our paths cross.
Stunned at this pumped up face you'll see;
Concealed
The shape of my face you fancied.

So I'm taking away that chance.
You, boyfriend of my tear-soaked dreams,
I've left. A trance
I'm under, as the clinic expands my seams.
I ask you forget Suzy, that's what I ask.

I was convinced that Nick wouldn't fancy me now that I was putting on so much weight. Fighting back tears, I pushed the letter into an envelope and started to copy out the address.

"Are you okay, Suzy?" asked Yun. She was looking at me in a concerned way.

"Yes, fine, thanks," I said quickly. I noticed that some of the others had brought down their duvets and pillows, as we were going to watch a film. I felt really stuffed from the macaroni cheese I'd eaten at dinner, so that it was painful even shifting position. But at least I'd managed to eat something vegetarian, instead of the corned beef hash that the others had to eat. After three weeks here, a dietician had told me that I could choose three foods to write on the clinic's Dislikes List: foods I wouldn't have to eat while I was here. I'd had a lot of trouble narrowing my dislikes down to just three though – and they couldn't be fish, chips or ice cream. I'd ended up choosing potato, crème brûlée and cheesecake.

Wyatt passed me a Diet Coke.

"Oh, thanks," I said, surprised and touched.

"Best hide it under the sofa," he said.

Tommy, one of the night nurses, came across to the telly and slotted a DVD into the machine below it. He was a hippie with a greying ponytail. He smiled over at us: "This is probably the best film that's been made about anorexia," he said.

I read on the screen, FEBRUARY 1983. Next the camera moved over a wall displaying platinum discs, and a poster of The Carpenters band, showing Karen and her brother Richard. Karen sang:

Talking to myself and feeling old.
Sometimes I'd like to quit,
Nothing ever seems to fit.
Hanging around, nothing to do but frown.

Now Karen was shown collapsed on the floor.

Rainy days and Mondays always get me down...
A silence had come over the room; everyone was still and I was hit by cold shock. *Why had I starved myself?*

I pulled my knees tighter towards my chest. *Anorexia could kill you.* I'd known this of course, but somehow it hadn't really sunk in before. Was the heart failure that Karen had suffered the same as had happened to *litebitetara*? I'd been so obsessed with calories and the weight I was gaining, there'd been barely space to spare any thought for her, but now I felt really guilty.

"You all right?" Wyatt asked.

I gave him a shaky smile, and said, "I guess it's really only just sunk in for me what can happen."

"You stupid, or what?" said Rihanna. "Why d'you think we're here unless we could die? People only pay for us to have treatment coz it's serious."

"Karen was thirty-two. It's young to die," Yun said gently.

After a long pause, Leah said, "This girl died in my last hospital. She was admitted late one night, and she looked awful. The doctors took her off to a side room. These alarms were ringing then. But it was only the next morning a nurse came and told me that she'd died."

"That's awful," Yun said.

Leah went on, "But the nurse said it in a way to try to shock me out of my anorexia...but anorexia's not simple like that."

Yun said, "It's weird but what really scares me about anorexia isn't dying, but getting health problems. It would be awful not being able to have kids. I want to have two or three kids when I'm older."

"And me," said Leah. "I've never even had a period."

I stared at Leah, out of shock. She was two years older than me. She couldn't know what it was like to have period pain. I saw periods as a big inconvenience. Still, I'd rather have them than not. They cleared up my skin, and also I wanted to have kids one day.

Maybe I was in shock, but my own situation now overwhelmed me. "I shouldn't die if I eat from now on, should I?" I asked the others desperately.

"Don't know," Rihanna said abruptly. "We're not doctors, are we?"

"You'll be all right, probably," said Yun. "You haven't had anorexia for that long. But you need to keep eating." She smiled at me.

"Thanks," I said gratefully. I swore to myself I'd eat properly from now on. *I didn't want to die!* But part of me still didn't want to put on weight, either.

“IT’S GETTING LIKE BIG BROTHER HERE.”

We were sitting on my bed. Leah and Rihanna were flicking through one of my magazines. Yun was downstairs having therapy.

“I think that model looks really good,” said Leah.

“Let’s see the picture,” I said.

Leah held up the magazine, showing a model in a purple dress, her red hair and porcelain-like face totally striking as she walked up a red carpet.

“She’s so lucky to be size zero,” I said.

“Suzy, you’re not far off that,” Rihanna said.

I smiled at Rihanna. I was so glad that she was being nicer to me today. I shouldn’t always jump to thinking that she had a low opinion of me. It made the ward feel like school, where I often used to feel I didn’t fit in.

“Who was that model who died from anorexia last month?” Leah asked.

“I can’t remember her name,” I said, remembering the newspaper article I’d read just the other day. "Apparently she hadn't eaten anything for weeks before she died at Fashion Week. Now lots of people are saying that the sizes models wear should be bigger."

"But it's not because of models that we get anorexic, is it?" said Rihanna. "I don't know about you, but my anorexia started because of my parents' divorce. They were arguing loads, and I got caught up in their arguments." She pulled a face.

I was surprised hearing this. Somehow I had thought that Rihanna was unaffected by other people.

"My parents separated too," said Leah. "But seriously, I think really thin models create the fantasy that if you're skinny, you'll be happy. I still feel that way sometimes." She stared into space, lost in thought.

"What about you, Suzy?" Rihanna asked me.

"I guess I just didn't want to be chubby any more," I said. "That's why I dieted."

"Well, I reckon clothes look better if the model's thin," said Rihanna, putting down the magazine. "Come on, let's go into Woodstock."

I was walking between Leah and Rihanna. It felt quite squashed on the pavement, and I was glad to reach the wider road. The small town was pretty boring, but at least we were out.

"Look, my friends have got fags," said Rihanna.

Two Goths were smoking on a bench in front of the town hall. Rihanna was already walking over. She was saying something I couldn't hear to the girl with the long glossy dark hair and pale face. She stubbed out her fag and got something out of her bag, as Rihanna sat on the empty seat beside her. I started to feel nervous.

"Hi Mel. These are my friends," Rihanna said, and she gave us a big smile.

"Hi," I said.

The girl was looking at us as if we were weird. But what about her? Her hair was dyed in chunks of pink and purple and her green and white stockinged legs stuck out from under her long dark trench coat. "You lot look like you need a meal," she said, touching up her black eyeliner.

"So? What's it to you?" said Rihanna, sounding really aggressive.

"Wow! No need to jump down our throats," said Mel. "I'm making you a rollie, for Christ's sake." Her fingers were really adept at rolling the paper round the baccy.

"Where d'you live?" Rihanna asked.

"Land of Oz," said Mel's friend. I noticed how bumpy her skin looked under her thick foundation.

"Let's hope you don't get swept up by the wind then," Rihanna replied sarcastically.

"Chill, Ella," said Mel to her friend, handing Rihanna the roll-up. "They're all right." She turned to face us again, and said, "You're living at that hospital down the road, aren't you? I think I've seen you walking down in that direction." There was an awkward silence, then she said, "Don't worry, I won't tell anyone. The place gives me the creeps; every time I've cycled past it's been locked.

"It is creepy," I said, thinking about how the place looked really bad.

"It's worse than prison," Rihanna said. She'd

opened a packet of the pills that she had bought earlier from the chemist's, and she swallowed a couple with a Diet Coke.

"What are those?" asked Leah quickly.

Rihanna didn't say anything, but she passed Leah the packet.

"Turboslim," Leah read out, and she looked impressed. "So that's why you made us wait outside the chemist."

Rihanna grinned at Leah.

"Can I have a couple of these?" Leah asked.

"You lot are crazy," said Ella.

I watched Leah swallow two pills without water, as she hated drinking any fluid she didn't have to. I felt annoyed that I hadn't sneaked into the chemist earlier to weigh myself. I'd decided against it, thinking that the others would grass on me to Penny.

"You want some?" Rihanna asked me.

I hesitated. "Okay, thanks," I said, and took the packet that Rihanna passed me.

"It's a shame you lot can't get out when you want," said Mel. "My brother's having a party tomorrow night, and he wants more girls to come."

"Yeah, it sucks," agreed Rihanna. "Still, we could meet you tomorrow afternoon. We've got passes then."

I had my therapy appointment then. I felt bitter and said nothing as they discussed meeting up again.

"She's okay," Rihanna said to Wyatt.

Okay for what? We were the only ones left in the lounge, and I started to feel curious and nervous at the same time. Yun was carrying in a jug of water, and she said quickly, "Come on, open the door."

"Okay," Wyatt said, as he opened the door for Yun to enter his room. "But Suzy, you'd better not tell anyone."

"I won't, I promise," I said. But I didn't know what I was promising not to say.

I followed the others into Wyatt's room, which was small but way tidier than mine had ever been. Rihanna and Leah were already in there, sitting on the bed. They grinned at us.

Yun said, "I've got apples and muesli, but only a couple of boxes, or Penny will get suspicious. And there's two jugs of water in Wyatt's cupboard, plus what I've got here."

Leah said, "Here's a bowl," and she handed one to me.

"Oh, thanks," I said, in a surprised way. "What do we do?" I asked.

"You've done tanking before?" asked Wyatt.

I shook my head.

"Virgin anorexic," said Rihanna laughing loudly. "Who's gonna explain to Suzy?"

"I will," said Wyatt. "Tanking means you eat as much cereal as you can. You then drink loads of water, and the cereal soaks it up. It can make you up to three kilos heavier than you actually are on the scales."

I was due to get weighed tomorrow morning. I smiled back at Wyatt now.

"It's a well tried and tested method," said Wyatt, grinning at me.

"So, do you want some muesli?" asked Yun.

I could see Rihanna watching me closely. "Yeah, sure," I said, holding out my bowl. *I'd never imagined before that I would eat extra calories here!*

There beside the back door was an oblong box, a longish foam microphone on a pole and some bags. I hadn't expected the filming to start so quickly. A woman who was the spitting image of Karen Carpenter entered the kitchen.

"This is Elizabeth," said Penny.

"Good morning, everyone," Elizabeth said.

She was skinny and smartly dressed in a brown jacket, jeans and elegant brown boots. Her carefully made up eyes were looking round at us, though she carried on smiling as if she wasn't shocked at all.

Penny said, "We're just finishing breakfast."

I ate another bite of buttery muffin slowly. I still couldn't believe that I hadn't been weighed that morning. Usually I got weighed on a Tuesday and a Friday. Last night in the end I'd eaten two bowls of cereal – *all for nothing!*

"I don't want to interrupt anything," Elizabeth said quickly.

"No, you're not. I'll put on some coffee," said Penny briskly. She switched on the kettle, and there was a roar as it boiled. "Elizabeth, do you take sugar?" asked Penny.

"No thanks. No milk either," she said.

Penny's face looked surprised, then she passed Elizabeth the mug. It wasn't fair because we weren't allowed coffee unless we had milk in it.

"Are you the film producer?" Wyatt asked Elizabeth.

"That's me, but we're not too formal about it, are we?" Elizabeth said, looking at the two men who had just entered the kitchen.

"No," they both said.

"We'd better introduce ourselves," said the shorter, stocky man with a beer belly. "I'm Graham, but you don't usually see much of me because I'm the one behind the camera. You can remember me because I'm the bald bloke."

"And I'm David," said the other man. "I do the sound." He brushed back his blond hair from his face, which had gone red. I noticed Leah and Rihanna smiling over at him, and both were blushing. *This was very unlike Rihanna.*

Elizabeth said, "I'm really bad at names unfortunately. Can you each say your name and something to help us remember you by?"

I waited for my turn, but I was really struggling to think of anything. "I'm Suzy. I like classical music, but not wailing opera."

It sounded totally corny, but Elizabeth and the men were smiling. I was the one who now felt my cheeks turn scarlet.

We sat in silence for most of the morning, unable to act naturally with the camera there. Lunch almost felt like a relief. Then I saw the paper bundles on the counter and remembered it was fish and chips Wednesday. I was being passed a plate, and the battered fish looked like it was swimming in grease. The chips were massive too. Leah had started to cry, everyone else was silent and, worst of all, the camera was aimed straight at me.

"We'll stop filming now, I think," Elizabeth said to Graham and David. "And take a break ourselves for lunch." They all went out, leaving us with our greasy food.

I let out a big sigh, and dug my knife into the fish. A stream of pus came out, but I still had to fork some into my mouth. *Picture Worthing. Eating in the café on the front with my grandparents and Ben. And laughing. Usually Ben or I had ordered a second bowl of chips to share. Crazy, it seemed now, after everything that had happened in the last year.* I stuffed into my mouth a chip that was too big, and started coughing. I took a long sip of water.

"Don't push any chips to the edge of your plate," Penny said. "It all has to be eaten."

"I know," I muttered.

She was telling Leah off then. *Ketchup and mayo I used to like on my chips. Then dessert – a knickerbocker glory that came served in the tallest glass. Down the bottom were strawberry and chocolate ice cream, while the top was squirted with cream and chocolate bits.*

The chips were gone. It wasn't that much longer before I could escape.

One knee on the toilet, the other leg hooked over the sink, I strained to see myself in the mirror. There were no full-length mirrors on the ward, but I could kind of see why that was. I took out of my left pocket my piece of string, a little notepad and pencil. I just hoped that my measurements hadn't gone up. I started by measuring my flabby thighs, because I hated them most. I wound the string round my left thigh, marking the circumference with my left finger, and picked up my ruler from the sink to measure the length of string against it. I heard a knock at the door.

"Suzy," shouted Penny. "Unlock that door, and don't flush the toilet!"

Slightly dazed, I hooked my leg back on the toilet and tried to get down quietly.

"Open that door, *now*!"

My heart thumping against my ribs, I walked across the room. But already the door was opening. She must have a master key!

"You've made yourself sick, haven't you?" Penny shouted. Bright red spots had appeared on her cheeks.

"No...I don't know how to," I said. Apart from anything else, I was really embarrassed because standing behind her was Elizabeth and the film crew. Penny was crossing the bathroom, and I watched as she flushed the toilet. "See, I told you," I said.

Penny said, "So why are you in here? You know you're not supposed to go to the bathroom for thirty minutes after a meal. The others have noticed you disappearing after meals, so I came to investigate."

Who had grassed on me?

"Today you had fish and chips, which I imagine you thought is fattier than the other meals."

"Well, I didn't make myself sick."

Penny ignored me, and turned to Elizabeth and the camera. "Anorexics sometimes try to make themselves vomit, thinking they will get rid of calories they don't want. It can cause many health problems."

"Like what?" Elizabeth asked.

"It can make their tooth enamel erode," said Penny. "Vomiting's very dangerous, as it reduces salt and ions, especially potassium, and these need to be kept in balance for the body to work properly. In severe cases, this can cause seizures or heart failure." Penny turned to me, and said, "Suzy, in future the bathroom will be locked for half an hour after meals."

I didn't say anything.

She crossed the bathroom, but paused beside the sink and bent down. "What's this?" she asked, dangling my piece of string in the air.

"Nothing," I said.

"Really? Is that right?" she said, a smile appearing on her face. "Well, I'll keep hold of it."

I stared as she locked the bathroom door. *What if people at school saw what had just been filmed, some day in a few months' time? It was a horrible thought.*

Joe wasn't saying anything much. I guessed that he wanted me to speak more, but I wouldn't. *A liar*, that's what Penny thought I was. She really thought I made myself sick, because the bathroom doors were all locked now after meals. And the others were really cross about this.

"You seem a bit distracted," said Joe. "Is there something you want to tell me?"

"Not really. Well, you wouldn't understand."

"Try me."

"It's like no one trusts anyone else here," I said, playing with my watchstrap. "So I'm constantly having to pretend everything's fine, yet worrying about whether I've done something wrong."

"Can you give me an example?" he asked.

"Otherwise it's hard to respond helpfully."

I tried to think of an example that I didn't mind him knowing about. I said, "Take the phone calls here. You're only supposed to talk to your family twice a week, but some of the others make more calls, well they seem to anyway," I said quickly. "And today I needed to ask my mum to post me more cello music, but Rihanna made a big thing to staff about how it wasn't fair I was phoning my mum a third time this week."

"It must be difficult living together here, as you're all in a place you'd rather not be. Is that right?"

I nodded.

"I imagine the others are missing their friends and family as well," Joe said, and paused. "I'm just suggesting that maybe you can make some allowances for the others."

"I'll try."

"That's good, Suzy," said Joe. "That brings us to something I wanted to mention. On Monday we'll be having the first family therapy session, so your mum, Rupert and Ben will be there. How do you feel about this?"

"Dunno...Guess I don't have much choice," I said.

Joe grinned at me, and said, "You might end up finding it helpful. See you on Monday."

I gave him a blank look. *I just wanted to go home!*

"Wow," Wyatt said to Yun. "So what are you going to do? Penny's going to go crazy when she finds out that you've exercised in your room."

"Dunno," said Yun. "It was Leah as well."

"Yeah, we were doing aerobics on the steps of their dresser," Leah said, and grinned.

I stared at her. Now I knew why Yun had moved my stuff off the dresser. I felt hurt that they hadn't asked me to join them.

It was feeling squashed on the landing, and already it was getting dark outside, though it was only six. It made our shadows look weird on the wall, like with fairground mirrors that make everyone look taller.

Yun went on, "I hope she doesn't put back the day I'm getting discharged."

"I reckon Penny's going to find out," said Wyatt. "She found out about me doing weights in the lounge, when they filmed that." And he sighed.

"At least we're not the only ones who've been caught," said Leah. "Rihanna was caught dancing in her room too. It's getting like Big Brother here."

"I heard Elizabeth telling Mike that she wanted us to open up more," Wyatt said. "This is hardly a way of gaining our trust."

"I know what you mean," I said. "I felt really dumb getting caught in the bathroom the other day. And I wasn't even doing anything."

"Sorry, we've been a bit harsh on you about it. It's just it's annoying all the bathrooms being locked after meals," said Wyatt.

"Doesn't matter now," I said.

"What are we going to do?" asked Yun.

"I'm not sure. We'd best ask Rihanna," said Wyatt, picking at a loose thread on his jumper. "She'll know what to do."

"She's with the Goths again," said Leah.

"Lucky the camera can't follow her there," said Wyatt, grinning.

"ALL I MEANT WAS THAT YOU LOOK HEALTHIER NOW."

"You can't take your towel in there," said Yun. "Give it to me."

I paused for a moment or two. I really couldn't have anyone seeing my jelly-thighs.

"Come on. The others will already be swimming."

Yun jammed the towel into the locker with her things. "Sorry, I didn't mean to snap," she said. She started to run across the slippery changing room floor towards the pool area.

"Thanks, Yun," I called after her.

I was sad that she was leaving the clinic in just a few days' time. Mike was at the side, still wearing his suit. "Suzy, you're allowed to do thirty lengths, but no more. Only backstroke or front crawl," he said, glancing at his watch. "You've got twenty-five minutes left."

Suddenly I didn't feel like getting into the pool. I dipped my foot into the water, which felt quite cold. I noticed the film crew standing at the window of the café area, and Graham was pointing the camera towards the other side of the pool. I saw the others all doing lengths, almost racing, like it was a competition. I started to worry that they were burning off more calories.

I decided it was best just to dive in. I pushed off the bottom of the pool and came up again, my ears popping loudly. I started doing front-crawl, but felt I was pulling my arms through thick treacle. I touched the end of the pool and turned round, just starting to enjoy myself, when I saw Leah crying at the side. *Should I stop? But I didn't want to. The others had swum loads of lengths already, and I needed to catch up with them.* Luckily, Mike was walking over to Leah, so I carried on swimming.

When I'd just got to twenty lengths, Mike blew the whistle and we had to get out.

"Did you enjoy it?" Yun asked. She wrapped her large towel tightly round herself.

So why had Yun told me that I couldn't take my towel in there? "Yeah, swimming again was great!" I said. I looked up at the window to see if we were still being filmed. But the film crew had gone, luckily.

"Is Leah all right?" I asked Wyatt.

"Dunno," Yun said, shaking her head. "She was having a panic attack."

We moved into the shower area, but the cubicles were all full.

"We'll have to use the communal one," said Yun.

"We should have come at a less busy time," said Rihanna, pulling a face.

I hated changing in front of the others, and it was taking ages. I needed to hold my towel up with one hand, while I peeled off my costume, which had stuck round my tummy like a damp fish.

"We're not going to look, if you're worried about that," said Yun, smiling.

I didn't want to talk to her after her lie about the towel. I said briskly, "I've always changed this way."

Luckily the others weren't listening, as they were having another conversation. Yun said, "I feel sorry for Leah. She must feel really bad to keep having panic attacks."

"She doesn't like the weight she's gaining," said Rihanna. "But who does? The pain has to come out some way. See this scar on my arm. It's been there two years."

I saw this spider-web white line stretching up her forearm, and I felt sick. "Didn't it hurt a lot?" I asked her.

Rihanna interrupted, saying, "You've never cut, have you?" She looked closely at my face, and there was a bright glint in her eye, which I didn't like. She went on, "Careful what you say. Cutting for me gets rid of this awful feeling I get inside sometimes, well for a bit."

That was when I noticed the thin red scars on her arms. How could I not have seen these before? But then, she often wore long tops and jumpers. "I'm sorry," I muttered.

But she didn't say anything as she pulled on her jeans over legs that were scarred too.

I wanted to run out of there, but I still had to change into my clothes. I dropped the towel, pulling off my costume quickly.

I was really anxious as I walked into the first family

therapy session. I didn't know what it was going to be like.

"Isn't she looking better, Dr Avery?" Mum said.

Bird Cage smiled and Rupert nodded his head encouragingly. But all Joe said was "Hi, Suzy." He must know that I felt really uncomfortable.

"By better you mean fatter, don't you, Mum?" I said.

"No, Suzy," said Mum. "All I meant was that you look healthier now." Turning back to Bird Cage, she said, "We're so grateful for all the help that you and the rest of the staff have given Suzy."

Penny entered and sat down next to Bird Cage on the sofa, so it felt like they were the bad cops, and Joe was the good cop, and I was the one about to be interrogated. I decided to adopt the policy that I, and the others, now had with the film crew and camera, which was to say nothing that could be twisted round.

"Ben, put your phone away!" snapped Mum.

Ben, sitting on an easy chair next to me, pulled a face.

"Thank you all for coming here today," said Joe. "The aim of these sessions is to explore how you can best help Suzy as a family."

"We desperately want to do that," said Mum. "It's broken my heart, Suzy getting so thin."

"Suzy means the world to Kath," said Rupert. "She would do anything for her."

"Kath," said Joe. "What can you remember about the time when Suzy started to lose weight? What we're interested in is thinking of possible triggers."

"It was in January she started losing weight," Mum said. "It was a New Year's resolution of Suzy's, I think, losing a bit," and she looked over at me anxiously. "But it was just puppy fat on her and I'm sure she would have grown out of it."

I hated her describing me like this!

Mum went on, "The trouble is that children can be cruel to each other. And sometimes she didn't want to go to school because of the bullying."

"What form did the bullying take?" asked Bird Cage.

"Mainly name-calling. But one of the girls was jealous of Suzy and gave her a food diary. I've shown it to Penny...what was her name?"

"Gemma," said Ben. "She's a real nightmare. But Nick, that's Suzy's boyfriend, and I have had words with Gemma. She'll be nice to Suzy from now on, or she's got us to answer to."

I glared at him.

"And did you speak to the school about the bullying, Kath?" asked Bird Cage.

Why all these questions from her? I'd only met her properly once before.

"I spoke to Suzy's form tutor, Mr Dewberry, on a couple of occasions," said Mum. "But now Suzy's ended up ill as a result, the matter's being taken very seriously by the school." Mum gave Bird Cage and Penny a meaningful look, as if to say that there was more to tell them later, when I wasn't listening.

Joe said, "Were any other events happening around this time which Suzy may have found difficult?"

"Suzy was doing a lot of music competitions," Mum said reluctantly. "She's the kind of girl who can't bear not to win something."

"Perfectionism's often a trait we find in children suffering from anorexia," said Bird Cage, and she noted something down in her file.

"Yeah, right, turn it on me, Mum," I said angrily. "You haven't told them that you're always telling me the mistakes I've made after a performance. You hardly ever praise me. Also, I bet they don't know that we hardly ever have family meals!" I shouted.

Mum hadn't expected this; there was an awkward pause, and she said, "That's because you eat at your grandparents before you're dropped back."

"Ben doesn't have to go there, so I don't see why I should. And I hate going to Granny and Grandpa's," I said quickly. It was a lie, but I didn't care. I just wanted to say something to make her look bad.

"Sorry, Suzy," said Rupert. "But Ben's sixteen. When you're sixteen, you'll be allowed to come back to the house directly after school." Rupert turned to the doctors, and said, "Kath and I don't finish work until seven, eight some evenings. We felt that while Suzy wasn't eating properly, her grandparents should supervise her dinners."

"Yes, that's sensible," said Penny.

"You're all ganging up on me!" I shouted. I now thought of my target weight. "I don't even want to be here. Now I'm being made to gain all this weight, by the time I get back to school everyone will laugh at me." I stood up, pushing the chair back.

"Suzy, we're not taking sides," said Joe, in a calm voice. "What would you like us to talk about?"

"Nothing! I'm sick of this!" I shouted.

"Don't shout, Suzy," said Mum, sounding embarrassed. "I can only apologise for Suzy's behaviour."

"Shut up!" I shouted, and stormed out.

Ben was the one who found me on the steps, where I sat crying. "It probably sucked being the one everyone talked about," he said.

"Yeah, when it's none of their business," I said.

"I forgot, I've got something for you," he said, giving me a present wrapped in silver paper. "It's from Nick. And this is from me." He passed me a plastic bag which was stuffed full of magazines.

"Thanks, Ben," I said, wiping my eyes with a tissue. "That's really nice of you." Looking inside, I saw favourites like *Bliss!* and *Marie Claire*.

"Amber said that these are the ones girls read," he said.

I flicked through *Marie Claire* and came to a diet. At least I could read this normally, when everything was pretty much censored here. "How's it going with Amber?" I asked Ben.

"Pretty good," he said, grinning. "I think she really likes me."

There was a sound, and I turned round to see Mum standing there, her eyes all red. "Okay now?" she asked.

"Not really," I said, hunching my shoulders.

"I do love you, Suzy," she said. "I don't know how to make you realise that."

Rupert was standing behind Mum, and said, "We both do, Suzy. This is difficult for all of us."

"Well, you're not the ones stuck here in prison, are you?" I said angrily, picking up the magazines and storming up the steps.

"Suzy!" Mum said, and tried to reach out towards me.

I pushed her away, and she stumbled on the step, clinging for the rail.

"Suzy, that's unacceptable!" shouted Rupert.

Mum was sobbing, but I didn't care. I ran up the rest of the steps and into the ward. *Why didn't Mum just get the message that I really hated her for making me stay here?*

Penny came into the kitchen holding a phone, but covering the mouthpiece with her hand. "Suzy," she said, "I've got a very persistent young man on the phone for you. He says that he absolutely has to speak to you, and it can't wait. Will you take it? But you have to be quick, as I'm serving lunch at 12 sharp."

Nick! It had to be him. "Okay," I said awkwardly, taking the phone from her. "Hello?" I said, walking with the phone across to a corner.

"It's great to hear you," said Nick. "I hope you don't mind me calling, but Ben told me he was visiting you today, so I thought I'd call when you're there and not doing more exciting things."

"Did you get my letter and poem?" I asked.

"Yes, and that's partly why I'm calling," he said. "I wanted to tell you that nothing's changed between us, and I still feel exactly the same way. I really miss you, Suzy."

Some of the others were coming into the kitchen, so it was difficult to talk. "You know I'll look different when I finally get out of here," I said.

"That's good," Nick said. "You were way too skinny. Have you opened the present from me?"

"Er, no," I said. "What is it?"

"Not telling. Open it," Nick said, and laughed.

"Suzy!" Fran said, and pointed to her watch.

"Nick, I've gotta go," I said. "We're having lunch early, because we're going on a walk with some wolves this afternoon."

"Wolves, wicked!" he said. "I didn't know they were that tame. Or are you going to offer the doctor to them?"

I laughed, but Fran was walking over towards me. "Bye, Nick." I said these words just in time, because the next second Fran was taking the phone from me.

"My boyfriend Nick still likes me," I said quietly to her.

Fran smiled, and said, "Course he does. You're a lovely girl."

It was a relief when the minibus door shut behind me. The big blow-up in therapy meant that Penny had nearly stopped me going to the Wolf Conservation Trust. The trip was to celebrate the fact that Yun had got to her target weight and was about to be discharged.

"It must have been nice seeing your family," said Yun.

"Not really," I said glumly. I twisted my finger round Nick's sweet present, which was a silver heart-shaped locket on a necklace hanging round my neck. *If only I could be round at Nick's house again!*

We'd reached the end of the ancient, sandy-coloured houses, and the minibus joined a busy road. It was the first time I'd left the place for weeks, and suddenly I felt jittery with excitement.

The silvery white wolf moved to a standing position,

and his powerful shoulders flexed as he stretched backwards onto his hind legs. His tail was like a fox's, but much bigger. He yawned, making his large pink tongue roll outwards.

"He's thinking it's time for his lunch," said Wyatt. And he grinned at us.

"His name's Kodiak. And you lot are quite safe," said the keeper from the pen, smiling at us. His wrinkled face looked relaxed. I wouldn't be nearly that calm if I was standing in there. He went on, "He's quite full up. I only fed him twenty minutes ago."

"What did he eat?" asked Wyatt.

"Raw chunks of beef."

"Gross!" said Rihanna. Yun looked disgusted as well.

"You're not going to make him vegetarian," said Wyatt, and he grinned.

"You don't say," said Rihanna sarcastically.

The wolf had walked over to the other side of the pen, and the keeper said, "You can't forget that they're wild animals. It's all right if Kodiak chooses to come over and see me, but I wouldn't go over to him. I have to respect his space."

"More than they do with us," said Wyatt, looking over at Elizabeth, who was walking over to us with Graham, carrying the camera, and David, holding the microphone.

"Yeah, well like I said, ignore them," said Rihanna. "They'll soon get the message then."

But wasn't that difficult if you had a camera pointing directly at you? I didn't say anything as I didn't dare; Rihanna seemed so snappy.

"So are you lot ready for the walk with the

wolves?" asked Wyatt. "They look so docile that you could stroke them, but then they'll turn on you and gobble you up!" He pounced on Yun, who shrieked loudly.

Everyone was laughing.

Mike was walking over with a young female keeper, who'd just given a really interesting talk about how the keepers cared for the wolves here. Her face was animated as she chatted to Mike, who was scanning us as he did a headcount. "Where's Leah?" he asked.

"Dunno. Maybe a wolf's eaten her," joked Rihanna.

Mike ignored the comment, and said, "Can the rest of you think where you last saw Leah, please?"

"It was in the shop," said Yun. She glanced at her watch. "It was about half an hour ago."

"Right, I'll go and look there," said Mike. "Can you all stay together here, please." He rushed off.

"I hope she's all right," said Yun, sounding anxious.

"Me too," I said.

Mike came back over with the bad news: "I'm afraid Leah's missing, and Penny wants us to wait in the minibus. She's notifying the police. And Fran is on her way over. When she gets here, I'll drive you lot back to the ward, and Fran will wait here in case Leah turns up."

Elizabeth said to Mike quietly, "Is there anything we can do?"

"Just keep an eye open, that's all," said Mike.

Elizabeth nodded, and said, "Of course."

I looked up at the fiery leaves on the branches. A wind had started to blow. It certainly wasn't a place where I'd want to go missing. I started to feel really scared for Leah.

TARGET WEIGHT

"So how did Leah get to Reading?" Yun asked Wyatt.

"Apparently she called a friend in Reading to pick her up," said Wyatt.

"At least she's safe," said Fran, sitting next to me at the table, sipping her coffee. "But it was irresponsible of that girl to pick her up without telling the clinic, when she knows she's under our care."

Rihanna said, "Is this being filmed?" The camera was quite close to her, and pointed in her direction.

Graham shook his head, and said, "No, it's not been switched on yet."

"Yes, we thought we'd wait until you'd started talking," said Elizabeth. "We want you all to feel relaxed in front of the camera before we do set pieces. Just try and forget we're here."

We didn't want to be filmed!

But no one said anything. Rihanna leaned towards Fran. "So what's gonna happen to Leah?"

"It's not a matter for you to concern yourselves with," said Penny, who had just walked into the kitchen, holding some files. "I'll be having that discussion with members of staff here." There was a loud ring on the doorbell. "I expect that's Leah," said Penny, in her firm voice. She went to answer it.

"I expect Leah's in big trouble," said Wyatt.

Yun said, "My mum and dad will be here soon. At least Leah got back before I go home, so I'll know she's all right."

Suddenly it sank in that Yun was really going home for good, while I was stuck here for several more weeks. And I felt really envious of her. *Why couldn't it be me?*

I watched as Yun got into the red Fiesta that her parents were giving her for her birthday. It had L plates on the back, ready for her driving lessons when she turned seventeen next month, and Wyatt and Rihanna had decorated the car with bright coloured balloons and streamers. It was obvious that Yun hadn't been expecting this send off, as she wiped away a few tears.

The engine started shakily, and Yun waved from the window. The gate was creaking open, and we started to run behind the car. There was a blast from the horn, and the car pulled out into the road and disappeared. I felt lost for a moment. Now Yun was gone, our room was my own. And I wasn't sure if I totally liked that idea.

Curiosity stopped me leaving. With Leah sitting on the sofa, talking to Wyatt, I wanted to know what was going to happen.

A cartoon was playing. I walked across to join them on the sofa, and tucked my legs up.

"I still can't believe you ran away," Wyatt said to Leah. "One moment you were there, and the next you'd gone."

"Yeah, I'd planned it," said Leah. "Coz I just don't want to reach my target weight, and Penny won't listen to what I say."

"You can't think Penny will change it," said Wyatt.

"No, that's why I'm going to get discharged early," said Leah. She looked seriously upset, but determined too. Like nothing anyone said would change her mind.

"But Penny never lets anyone negotiate their weight," I said.

"I hate the way I look, and I've still got two kilos to gain," said Leah. "My mum understands that. We both think that I shouldn't have to put on any more, when I've already gained twelve kilos. But Penny won't listen."

I had this feeling that things would be getting uncomfortable, even dangerous for Leah soon.

"I think you should stay," said Wyatt.

"Me too," I said.

Leah took no notice, and she said, "I'm sick of this place."

I felt out of my depth. I got up off the sofa and left.

"Suzy, can I have a word?" Joe asked me. He walked up to where I was standing sipping water in the kitchen. My therapy session wasn't until tomorrow, and I was racking my mind as to why he wanted to see me early.

"We'll go in a different room today," he said.

I followed him into a large office.

"You seemed very upset the other day in the family therapy, before you walked out. I wanted to check that you were all right."

"I'm okay," I said. "I just didn't want to be there."

"I could see that," said Joe. "Your mum phoned me to say that you were very angry with her afterwards, and she'd found that hard to cope with. I think she feels that communication's broken down between the two of you. Is that right?"

"Yeah, well it's her problem."

"Is it?"

I was amazed that he was speaking so calmly.

There was a knock on the door, and Fran came in. "Sorry to interrupt, but we've got an emergency with a new admission. Can I have your help, Joe, for a few minutes?" she said.

Joe followed Fran through to the corridor. I wondered what the problem could be.

"Sorry about that interruption," said Joe when he got back. I waited for him to say what had happened, but he just said, "Suzy, I think you're starting to feel really angry, and I want to explore the reasons for this. You know it's all right to feel angry."

"I'm just sick of everyone blaming me for stuff."

"Yes, but I think you're also angry about the pressures you've been under. Was it these that led to you deciding to diet, to make you feel noticed? Right?"

"I dunno...maybe," I said. But the word *noticed* had made me feel worried. "It wasn't attention-seeking, my diet," I said quickly.

"Does it worry you that others may think it was?"

"No...well, a bit," I said.

Joe smiled, and said, "You know we all need to feel noticed. It seems to me that at the time you started dieting, you were struggling to feel you were accepted as being your own person, and not just for the different things you were achieving. Dieting was a way of getting people to see you."

"Yes, that's right," I said. He really could see inside my head, into the stuff I found really difficult.

Joe looked up at the clock.

"We'd better leave it there today. I'll see you at the usual time next week."

I walked down the corridor. There were voices shouting in the kitchen, and someone was sobbing. *Real drama.*

Wyatt appeared a few moments later.

"What's happening?" I asked him.

"That new girl Anna's refusing to eat," Wyatt said. "Now, Penny's not letting us go to the cinema tonight, coz she's said it's got too unsettled here."

I carried on walking and turned into the second smaller lounge that nobody used much. But Rihanna and Leah were sitting on a sofa with Elizabeth, who was pointing to a magazine.

Rihanna spotted me, and said, "Suzy. Where've you been? You missed seeing Anna chuck her pizza at the wall."

"I've been seeing Joe," I said, and sighed.

Rihanna went on, "Well, you're lucky you have the fittest therapist. Joe's gorgeous."

"Yes, and you don't have to put up with my therapist, Maureen," said Leah. "I hate her!"

"This is the right place," said Rihanna. She had stopped at the edge of the garden, where we could just see the trees thinning out in the near darkness. There was no wall here, just a fence. "I think I can hear them."

She was knocking on the fence, and I was wondering if it was some secret code between her and the Goths.

"Won't Penny hear?" I asked nervously.

"Are you a pussy?" asked Rihanna. "Go back into the clinic if you want. But I said I'd meet Mel and Ella here. Penny's in a meeting with Bird Cage and the therapists, isn't she?" Rihanna went on, "They'll be discussing us for ages. All the catching out they've done lately, and thinking of more traps to set for us."

"Ah, shit," Rihanna exploded as she caught her cardigan on a thorny bush. She knocked on the fence again, and this time there was a dull thudding from the other side. "Hey guys," said Rihanna. "Are you there?"

"Just about. This bag you've asked us to bring is heavy." I recognised Mel's voice. "It's been a whole workout carrying it here."

"So how are we going to give it to you?" asked Ella.

"I'll climb up on the tree stump and you pass it to me," said Rihanna. "I need some light, Suzy." I shone Rihanna's torch over the stump, and Rihanna immediately started getting up there.

"Hey, Suzy, take this from me," said Rihanna.

The bag I took from her was heavy. My hand was pressed against the side pocket. It felt like there could be razor blades in there. But I didn't dare say anything, as Rihanna took the bag from me.

"Did you take a couple of packets of fags, like I said you could?" Rihanna said.

"Nah, don't worry about it," said Mel. "We figured we could buy our own and you're stuck in there."

"Well, thanks," said Rihanna, sounding quite touched. "Look, I'll see you tomorrow, where we said we'd meet."

We were about to cross the lawn, when suddenly the security light came on. "Oh, shit," said Rihanna.

We froze. Lit by the clinic's security light we saw Fran walking down the path.

"We can't move from here," whispered Rihanna.

So we were stuck there for several long minutes, not moving. I felt really cold without my coat, but I didn't feel I could moan about it.

Rihanna said quietly, "D'you want some more Turboslim? Coz you can if you want some."

I felt like this was a test. Was I a proper anorexic like her, or not?

"Well, if that's all right?" I said.

"Sure it is," she said, passing me the packet. "Come on, there's no one around."

And we hurried across to the ward, and into the warm.

Leah and her mum had been carrying her things downstairs all morning. We all thought we'd persuade her to stay, so it felt really weird lining up beside the back door to say goodbye. Rihanna and Leah hugged each other.

“Make sure you write to us,” said Rihanna.

“I’ll try,” Leah said. “Though I’m not much good at writing letters.”

It was my turn. I hugged Leah, and struggled to think of words to say. “Take care. I hope it goes okay,” I said. Tears pricked my eyes, and I bit my lip.

“It’ll be fine,” she said defensively. “I’ve got a better chance of getting well at home.”

“Have you?” asked Wyatt.

“Yes,” Leah said. “Coz at home I won’t be arguing with Penny all the time.”

“What about your mum?” Wyatt asked.

“We won’t argue,” said Leah.

I could tell that Leah didn’t want to hear anything else, as she quickly hugged Wyatt. I watched her wave at us all again and open the door. She stepped out into the cold wearing just a purple T-shirt, probably so she’d burn up more calories just keeping warm.

When the door was firmly closed, Wyatt said, “Well, I’ll give her three months before she’s back in hospital. Only the next place will be far worse than this.”

NOTHING'S THE SAME

"Suzy, do you mind if we film you watching the DVD from your school?" asked Elizabeth.

I didn't want this to happen; but perhaps because I wasn't used to making decisions these days, I found it difficult to say no.

"Go on, let's," said Rihanna.

"Your form must like you a lot to make a film for you," said my new roommate Anna. She had curly brown hair and brown eyes. But her cheekbones stuck out so much that even I found her gross to look at.

I smiled weakly back at her.

Anna reached for a cushion and sat on top of it; the floor must have felt too hard without a cushion.

"Can you turn the lights down, Rihanna, please?" asked Elizabeth.

In the weeks here it was almost like my form had stopped existing for me, I'd pushed thoughts of them so far away. So what came next was more than I could cope with.

The film showed my form and Mr Dewberry

waving, and everyone saying, "Hi, Suzy!"

Molly and Carla were standing outside the form room, smiling.

Carla said, "It's taken us ages to make this film, coz everyone mucks around..."

Adam now ran behind them, pulling faces.

Rihanna and some of the others laughed.

Molly went on, "But we thought if we couldn't see you, we'd make a film of the more entertaining stuff that's been happening at school."

"But school's pretty boring," said Carla quickly.

She actually sounded genuine, and I bit my lip.

There was a shot of the history classroom next, and Molly scribbling in her exercise book. She looked up, grinning at the camera. "Hey, Suzy! Like usual, I'm doing my homework at the last minute. Actually, better not have that bit on camera." She laughed.

The camera moved again.

"Nick?" Molly called after him.

He turned round from his group of friends, and he went scarlet. He always got really shy around cameras. Nick looked lost for words, and said, "Hi, Suzy!"

Adam thumped him on the back, and said, "Suzy, do us all a favour and get back quick. Nick doesn't shut up about you, and he's driving us all mad.

My cheeks were now glowing as well.

But I wasn't prepared for who I saw next. Gemma. She couldn't see herself being filmed, and her uniform made her look surprisingly ordinary. Still, she was standing with Hannah at the picnic bench, chatting to some of Nick's friends.

"That's her!" I said to Rihanna.

"Who?" she said.

"Gemma, the girl who bullied me," I said. I'd already told Rihanna that Gemma used to pick on me at school, but I hadn't mentioned the food diary. I didn't want Rihanna guessing that I still kept a food diary.

"Her? The one with the nasty pleated skirt?" said Rihanna. "She looks a bitch."

I smiled. I liked the fact that Gemma was making such a poor impression on Rihanna.

Then I remembered that we were being filmed, and dread filled me. After the film ended, I said, "It was nice of my friend Molly to make the film, but I'm not looking forward to going back to school."

Fran said, "Why's that, Suzy?"

"I've put on loads of weight, and I used to get bullied at school for being chubby," I replied.

Fran said, "I'm sorry to hear that. Maybe I could ask you all a question. How many of you felt like you fitted in at school?"

The room was silent. No one put their hand up. Evidently this was something we all had in common.

Anna spoke up. "I also got teased at my school for being chubby. All the other girls were skinny, so I suppose I wanted to be like them."

Rihanna said, "I've heard my niece saying that she talks about diets at her school, and she's only six."

The terrible thing was that no one seemed shocked, and we all had similar examples. Everyone spoke at once.

"I was teased and bullied, so I stopped eating."

"If you were fat you were nobody."

"Suzy, be sensible!" Mum snapped. "If you move schools, there's no guarantee that your problems won't follow you there."

I stared down at my hands knotted together in my lap. Sensible. Why was it that now I'd got anorexia, my mind was somehow faulty? And Penny, Bird Cage, maybe even Joe too, were all taking notes in this stupid therapy. Couldn't they see that I didn't want to go back to a school where everyone had teased me when I had been chubby?

"And I can't afford to educate you privately, like your cousins, if that's what you're asking?" Mum said.

"I wasn't," I said, shrugging my shoulders.

Suddenly I felt really angry. "There's something else too," I said. "Mum, I want to find my dad. You must have some information."

Mum's face clouded.

"Look, Suzy, I've told you before that I don't know where he is."

"There must be something to go on," I pleaded.

"Kath, do you think you can help Suzy?" Joe asked.

"I'll have a look for my old address book," Mum said, in a quiet voice.

I felt a wave of satisfaction. And I wasn't even sure if I really wanted to see my dad. He hadn't wanted to see me, had he?

Sharing with Anna was taking some getting used to. She was way messier than I was. Her clothes, magazines and other things got dumped almost anywhere in our room. She wasn't chatty and easy-going like Yun had been, either. In fact, Anna barely spoke to me, and I worried that she didn't want to share with me.

Anna wasn't allowed to take part in activities or any exercise yet, so the only times that I really saw her was when she looked stony-faced at mealtimes, or was moaning in the telly room afterwards about feeling bloated. Given that Anna was on Obs, with staff checking up on her every fifteen minutes, she spent most of her time in the telly room. This meant that I had our bedroom to myself when I popped up there sometimes, which I was pleased about.

So when I walked into our bedroom one evening to find Anna sat on her bed crying, I felt really uncomfortable. I went to sit down beside her, and put my arm round her.

"What's the matter?" I asked her.

"It's Penny – she caught me being sick in the bin," Anna blurted out. Then she started sobbing again.

I leant over to reach for some tissues to give her.

"Now Penny is locking the bathrooms," Anna replied. "And I still don't have any leave. I can't even go for a walk."

I remembered how trapped I'd felt during my first few days here. "That sucks," I replied. I racked my mind for something to say to cheer Anna up. "Are your family visiting?" I asked her.

"No...not yet," Anna replied. "I'm only allowed to speak to them on the phone."

"It was like that for me too, for the first few days that I was here," I said. "Hey – do you want to see some photos?" I thought I'd show Anna some photos of Nick and my friends at home. It was a way of showing her that there was a life to get better for, because Anna must have friends at home too - perhaps a boyfriend as well.

Anna was crying again, so I went over to my chest of drawers to pull out the photo album that Nick had posted to me. I opened it at the photo of me playing a solo on the cello; I remembered it was Mendelssohn's 'Song Without Words'.

Anna was sniffing and dabbing her eyes with her tissue, but she took in the photo, asking, "Is that you?"

"Yes, I was playing a solo with my Youth Orchestra." But Anna looked rather blank. Maybe she didn't recognise me because I'd weighed a lot more in that photo? It was taken in the spring, before I'd gone on the crash diet.

"I don't play an instrument," said Anna. "But I like horse-riding, or I did before I got bulimia. My mum hasn't let me go riding for a few months. She says that I'm too skinny, and that if I fall off a horse I might break something."

"I like horse-riding, too," I said, and flicked over the pages to find the photo of me hugging Nick's horse Polo, but looking skinny by then. Nick stood to my right, grinning.

"Who's he?" asked Anna.

"My boyfriend," I said, feeling chuffed that I had a boyfriend who was as good-looking as Nick.

"I had a boyfriend too, until the bulimia started," said Anna, looking sad. "Then I kept cancelling my dates with him, coz in the evening all I wanted to do was take food up to my room and binge on it. Then I'd make myself sick."

I now remembered how anorexia had got such a

grip of me in the summer. "Anorexia's a bit like that too," I replied. "I'd lie to Nick and my friends that I had chores or cello practice to do after school, then I'd secretly exercise."

Anna smiled at me, and there was a knowing look in her eyes. We both understood each other, and I felt in that moment that we would become friends.

"Rihanna, wait!" Fran called after Rihanna.

"No, leave me alone!" Rihanna shouted. She nearly collided with the door, then started sobbing and kicked a chair against the wall. I hadn't seen Rihanna ever get upset like this. Fran pressed a button on the wall.

Wyatt entered the room. "What's the matter?" he asked.

"Someone's taken my ring and my money, that's what!" shouted Rihanna. "There's a thief here, but no one's going to admit to anything, are they? You're all a bunch of cowards."

I exchanged uncomfortable glances with Wyatt.

"Rihanna, don't take it out on the others," Fran said.

"Why not? Someone's taken my stuff," Rihanna shouted. "Whoever's done this is going to regret it."

Penny charged in, followed by Mike. It must have been an emergency button Fran had pressed, I thought.

"Rihanna, you need to calm down now," Penny said. "Your anger's getting over the top."

"Yes. I think you need some time on your own," said Fran.

"But what are you going to do about my stuff?"

asked Rihanna.

"You have to be responsible for your own possessions," said Penny. "Remember, it's a clinic. This is why you each have a locker for valuables to be locked inside."

Rihanna looked furious and she started sobbing again.

"Let's look through your room, Rihanna, to check your things aren't there," said Penny.

"They're not!" she shouted. "Search other people's rooms."

"Yes," said Penny. "But you first need to be calmer in order for us to do that. Mike, can you take Rihanna into the kitchen for a drink of water?"

Mike put his hand on Rihanna's shoulder, as Penny handed Fran see-through plastic gloves to put on. I knew they wore these for spot-checks of our rooms.

Rihanna turned round to me. "Suzy, you were near my room when I was having a shower," she said. "Did you see anything?"

"No," I said quickly.

"But Suzy, it was just you up here, wasn't it?"

She was suggesting that I was the thief! "Yes," I said. The silence that followed was very strained, broken by Mike saying, "Come on, Rihanna. Let's get that glass of water."

Rihanna glared at me.

Wyatt and Anna were laughing on the sofa. They were playing cards, but their bodies were really close together. Anna smiled at me, as I entered. We were getting on a lot better.

"Can I get the remote control?" I asked them.

I used the remote to flick between channels, but there was nothing good on. I went to the kitchen instead.

Wow, Zoe was back, talking to Mike. She looked really smart in her black trousers and grey, white and black stripey jumper. She must be back for a follow-up appointment, I thought.

"Hey, Zoe!"

"Hey," she said, but I could tell from her glazed look that she didn't recognise me. Zoe hadn't seen me since shortly after I'd been admitted to the ward.

"It's Suzy," I said.

"Oh, Suzy, sorry – I'm being stupid, aren't I? She came over and gave me a hug. "How are you getting on?"

"All right," I said. It had clicked that she hadn't recognised me because of my massive weight gain.

"That's good," she said, smiling, and turned back to Mike.

Why did I have to look different now? Not skinny like Anna, or that new girl Nancy who had arrived today. Okay, Nancy was only nine, but she was absolutely minute. I'd seen her sitting in the kitchen with a pizza in front of her. Penny was sitting next to her, encouraging Nancy to eat a chocolate bar. *I really hated how my shape had changed!*

"That's my seat, Suzy. My jumper's there," Wyatt said.

We'd got back into the minibus to eat our packed teas after stretching our legs. Anna wasn't with us. The ghost tour was just for those of us who could be trusted with eating outside the clinic.

I was passed a plastic bag that contained a tuna mayo roll, a Kit-Kat and a carton of orange juice. I guessed that the bag was plastic so that you couldn't hide anything in it.

"Everyone needs to take a bag of crisps, please," said Mike.

By the time this second plastic bag reached me, I was left with boring Ready Salted. I was angry about this as well.

We were all silent. I unpeeled the cling film off the roll and took a bite. I'd better hurry up, as I didn't want to make the others late for the ghost tour. Then I saw Wyatt, who was sitting to my left, wiping some of the buttery mayo onto a tissue and stuffing it up his sleeve. He smiled quickly at me, like nothing had happened.

I looked away. *I had thought that he was getting better!*

"The interesting thing about these ghosts is that they grow older," the tour guide said, in a bunged up voice.

"So don't the ghosts die then?" Rihanna asked. "They'd surely get cancer or something. Everyone dies."

I could tell that she was taking the piss, but the tour guide, who was quite young and enthusiastic, now looked impressed. He had a curious look on his face again, as he glanced across at Trinity College through the evening dusk.

"That's a very good point," he said. "There haven't been any sightings of the ghosts for some years. So they may actually have died."

I felt a tickling on my back and nearly jumped. "It's Banquo's ghost," Wyatt said, grinning.

I tried to smile to hide how freaked out I felt.

Then, the same thoughts started rolling round my mind again. *How could Wyatt have hidden some of his roll? I guess I'd thought that he was further along the recovery journey than me, now that he was going to a local boarding school for lessons in the daytimes.*

We trudged down the middle of the wide street and stopped at a bricked cross in the middle of the road. It was some kind of memorial.

"Suzy, mind the bicycle," said Mike briskly.

I stepped closer towards the group. It made me nervous, these bicycles rushing past us in the dark. The tour guide was still talking, and we had been standing here for ages. We moved on again, and Wyatt caught up with me. "You won't say anything about what you saw earlier?" he asked quietly.

"No, don't worry about it," I said.

Wyatt looked really awkward and said quickly, "It was only because I really don't like the taste of all that butter. I usually eat everything."

I didn't know what to believe any more.

A THIEF

I searched through my drawers again. I was sure that my purse had been in the top drawer – where was it? Now I had no money to buy stamps when I went to the shop with Rihanna. I needed stamps to send my letters to Nick, Molly and my grandparents. I ran my hand behind the chest of drawers, in case my purse had dropped behind. Then I got down on my knees to search under the bed. My purse was nowhere to be seen.

Feeling really stressed, I ran down the stairs and went to join Rihanna, who was waiting for me on the drive. I said, "I can't find my purse. Can I borrow some money to buy stamps?"

"Yeah, okay," Rihanna replied. "You know, some money and my ring went missing from my room, too. I reckon that new girl Anna's nicked our things."

"What?" I replied. "You're joking!"

"Come on, let's go," Rihanna said. "We've only got half an hour before we have to be back for lunch. And I want a run."

We let ourselves out through the gate, and I

walked fast to keep up with Rihanna. "So what do we do about Anna?" I gasped, now out of breath.

"I'll look through her things later, and see if I can find my ring," said Rihanna. But I reckon she'll have spent the money on food for binges and laxatives. She's bulimic, isn't she?"

"Yes, I know," I said miserably. "I wish I didn't have to share a room with her any more."

We reached the corner of the road and crossed to the cycle track under cover of the trees. We were still walking so fast that I was glad to be burning off calories.

When we came back into the lounge, I could see Penny checking Nancy's heartbeat with a red stethoscope. She must be dangerously ill; sicker than I had been, or Anna even. Nancy looked so drawn and ill that my eyes welled up.

Penny looked across at me, as if to say, *Don't be scared!* "Why don't you two have a chat together?" she said gently.

So I sat down next to Nancy as Penny left the room.

"I don't think we've really chatted much yet. What kinds of things do you like to do when you're not here?"

Nancy's face looked more like a mask, it was so deathly, but I did my best to ignore that.

"Well, I like playing the flute a lot, but my mum can't bring it until I'm better," said Nancy, looking sad.

"I play the cello," I said. "So when you're a bit better, we could play a duet perhaps."

"Really?" Nancy's face brightened up.

"Yes...I'm sure I could get hold of some music for flute and cello. There must be some," I said, and paused, thinking that I'd ask Julia to send some. "Or otherwise we can improvise."

"What's that?" Nancy asked me.

For a few moments I'd forgotten that Nancy was only nine, so I said quickly, "It's when you let the notes take you in their direction. You kind of make the music up as you go along."

Nancy looked dazed still.

So I went on, "Have you ever started to play the flute with the piano, and suddenly the piano changes key, say to a really sad tune. Well, when you improvise it's like that – you follow the other player, then they follow you."

"That sounds fun," said Nancy. She looked happier, and for a moment there was a sparkle in her green eyes. I had a sense of what a pretty girl she must have been when she wasn't so deathly thin, with those unusual eyes, and her dark curly hair and nice features.

I smiled, and said, "So that's a deal. But it means you'll have to eat more, coz I'm guessing that you don't have the energy to play the flute when you're so weak."

Nancy's face froze, and she looked nervously over to the door. *Maybe she was worried that Penny might walk in and overhear this?*

"Look, I need to go and ask if I can call my mum," she said, going out just as Wyatt entered with a big grin on his face.

"What is it?" I asked him.

"Anna's got a plan," Wyatt said. "She thinks we

should all have a massive water tanking session tonight."

"You've told her that we all do that?" I said, feeling angry. I'd been here a month before I was included in this; now that I knew that Anna was nicking money, I didn't want her joining in.

"Yes," replied Wyatt. "She thinks we should raid the kitchen cupboards more, to really bump up our weights before weigh-in."

I caught sight of Anna looking pleased over near the doorway. She looked away as I left the room.

I was on extra calories, because I hadn't gained a kilo last Friday when I got weighed. It had a lot to do with the fact that I hadn't joined in the recent water tanking session. This wasn't just because I didn't want to spend time with Anna. It was mainly because Penny had started to weigh people randomly, and I really didn't want to get caught and have my weekend leave cancelled.

In the kitchen, Nancy was crying as she stared at a buttered muffin. I couldn't believe how awful she looked, so much worse than two days ago. Penny and Fran were sitting next to her, with serious looks on their faces.

"Go on, take just one bite," said Fran.

"You really do need to try," said Penny.

Nancy said nothing.

I tried to encourage Nancy, but I felt really awkward. "I'm eating a chocolate bar now," I said.

"Okay, that's good Suzy," said Fran. "Take a Twix or Snickers from the bag on the counter. Come and sit at the table with us to eat it."

I decided on a Twix and sat down, peeling open the wrapper. My mouth full of chocolate, I tried not to stare at Nancy. She looked like a living skeleton.

Penny looked up. "Suzy, you have therapy with Joe starting in a minute."

I wanted to make some excuse as to why I couldn't see him, but if I started making excuses, Penny might not let me go to aerobics.

I walked into the therapy room and stopped in surprise. The chairs were arranged in the middle of the room in a circle, and Joe sat opposite where I stood. "It's like musical chairs," I said, giggling.

Joe motioned me to sit on a wicker chair opposite him.

"I don't want to get to my target weight," I blurted out. "I've listed the pros and cons of getting to target weight, and the cons outweigh the pros. You can read why." I took the crumpled list out of my pocket and thrust it at him.

Joe read it carefully. "That's good, Suzy, but I think you're still avoiding something very important. You may be able to decide logically what would be best, but that's different from deciding that you really want to change."

"I guess I do sometimes – other times I don't."

"Go on."

"Well, I don't want to go back to my old school. I I searched through my drawers again. I was sure that my purse had been in the top drawer – where was it? Now I had no money to buy stamps when I went to the shop with Rihanna. I needed stamps to send my letters to Nick, Molly and my grandparents. I ran my hand behind the chest of drawers, in case my purse had dropped behind. Then I got down on my knees to search under the bed. My purse was nowhere to be seen.

Feeling really stressed, I ran down the stairs and went to join Rihanna, who was waiting for me on the drive. I said, "I can't find my purse. Can I borrow some money to buy stamps?"

"Yeah, okay," Rihanna replied. "You know, some money and my ring went missing from my room, too. I reckon that new girl Anna's nicked our things."

"What?" I replied. "You're joking!"

"Come on, let's go," Rihanna said. "We've only got half an hour before we have to be back for lunch. And I want a run."

We let ourselves out through the gate, and I walked fast to keep up with Rihanna. "So what do we do about Anna?" I gasped, now out of breath.

"I'll look through her things later, and see if I can find my ring," said Rihanna. But I reckon she'll have spent the money on food for binges and laxatives. She's bulimic, isn't she?"

"Yes, I know," I said miserably. "I wish I didn't have to share a room with her any more."

We reached the corner of the road and crossed to the cycle track under cover of the trees. We were still walking so fast that I was glad to be burning off calories.

When we came back into the lounge, I could see Penny checking Nancy's heartbeat with a red stethoscope. She must be dangerously ill; sicker than I had been, or Anna even. Nancy looked so drawn and ill that my eyes welled up.

Penny looked across at me, as if to say, *Don't be*

scared! "Why don't you two have a chat together?" she said gently.

So I sat down next to Nancy as Penny left the room.

"I don't think we've really chatted much yet. What kinds of things do you like to do when you're not here?"

Nancy's face looked more like a mask, it was so deathly, but I did my best to ignore that.

"Well, I like playing the flute a lot, but my mum can't bring it until I'm better," said Nancy, looking sad.

"I play the cello," I said. "So when you're a bit better, we could play a duet perhaps."

"Really?" Nancy's face brightened up.

"Yes...I'm sure I could get hold of some music for flute and cello. There must be some," I said, and paused, thinking that I'd ask Julia to send some. "Or otherwise we can improvise."

"What's that?" Nancy asked me.

For a few moments I'd forgotten that Nancy was only nine, so I said quickly, "It's when you let the notes take you in their direction. You kind of make the music up as you go along."

Nancy looked dazed still.

So I went on, "Have you ever started to play the flute with the piano, and suddenly the piano changes key, say to a really sad tune. Well, when you improvise it's like that – you follow the other player, then they follow you."

"That sounds fun," said Nancy. She looked happier, and for a moment there was a sparkle in her green eyes. I had a sense of what a pretty girl she must have been when she wasn't so deathly thin, with those unusual eyes, and her dark curly hair and nice features.

I smiled, and said, “So that’s a deal. But it means you’ll have to eat more, coz I’m guessing that you don’t have the energy to play the flute when you’re so weak.”

Nancy’s face froze, and she looked nervously over to the door. *Maybe she was worried that Penny might walk in and overhear this?*

“Look, I need to go and ask if I can call my mum,” she said, going out just as Wyatt entered with a big grin on his face.

“What is it?” I asked him.

“Anna’s got a plan,” Wyatt said. “She thinks we should all have a massive water tanking session tonight.”

“You’ve told her that we all do that?” I said, feeling angry. I’d been here a month before I was included in this; now that I knew that Anna was nicking money, I didn’t want her joining in.

“Yes,” replied Wyatt. “She thinks we should raid the kitchen cupboards more, to really bump up our weights before weigh-in.”

I caught sight of Anna looking pleased over near the doorway. She looked away as I left the room.

I was on extra calories, because I hadn’t gained a kilo last Friday when I got weighed. It had a lot to do with the fact that I hadn’t joined in the recent water tanking session. This wasn’t just because I didn’t want to spend time really worrying about the others teasing me. That’s when I start thinking more about my weight and the calories I’m eating.”

"But getting teased is something you're already imagining will happen. It may not."

"But it might."

"What would they tease you about?" asked Joe.

"My weight, of course – I'm chubby again." I rushed on. "Like I was when they teased me before."

Joe looked thoughtful, and said, "But you're stabilising your weight at the average weight for a girl of your height and age," he said. "Do you think that half the girls in your school are fat?"

"Well, no," I admitted reluctantly.

Joe went on, "Let's hope the others at your school will have learnt what harm they can do by picking on someone's weight; that should be obvious from what's happened to you recently." He paused for a few moments, then continued. "But if they do say anything that's negative, it's your choice either to listen to them, or else reject the comments as what they are, unhelpful."

"I guess so," I conceded.

"People don't always say and do things we want them to. In life there can be setbacks. It's about learning to ride these."

I stared down at the rug, feeling miserable.

The next day, late afternoon, I finished my cello practice in the classroom and carried my cello into the clinic. When I came in to the lounge, most of the others were looking miserable. "Why's everyone in here?" I asked.

"Nancy's been transferred to the general hospital," said Wyatt. "I suppose staff were too concerned about her deterioration to keep her here any longer."

"How does that make you feel?" asked Elizabeth, sitting on the sofa next to him. I saw that the camera was rolling.

"Well, crap," said Wyatt. "She's only nine."

"I guess she's got to decide herself that she wants to eat, and that's the problem," I said.

Wyatt looked over at me, and said, "Suzy, you've got the big violin."

"Play us something, if you'd like to," suggested Elizabeth.

"Okay, I will," I said. Suddenly an idea occurred to me – I'd play Minsky's 'The Train Whistle'.

I sat down, tightened my bow, and launched into the noise of the train's screeching whistle. Then, with staccato bowing mixed with heavy down-bows, I made the sound of the train chugging along the rails.

When I finished, there was loud applause from the others.

"That was great," said Elizabeth. "A good way to finish filming for the day."

"Yes, we enjoyed it," said Graham, and David smiled too. Then the guys and Elizabeth went out. It was sad to think that filming would finish in just a few days. We didn't say anything else, as Anna entered the room. She went to sit down beside Wyatt, and he put his arm round her.

"What are you lot talking about?" she asked.

"Oh, nothing much," Wyatt said.

"It was me, wasn't it?" she said, looking upset.

"So what if it was?" snapped Rihanna.

Anna didn't say anything. I hadn't felt able to say anything to her until now about her nicking my money. It was not as if I, or Rihanna, had any proof.

When we'd searched through Anna's things, we hadn't found our money or Rihanna's ring. For the last couple of days I'd blanked Anna. But now my anger bubbled over, and I blurted out, "Anna, it was you who took my purse, wasn't it? And after I've tried to be nice to you."

"And you took my money! And my ring! I love that ring," shouted Rihanna.

Before anyone could say anything else, Anna ran out of the room and Wyatt followed her.

"He's only taking her side because he fancies her," muttered Rihanna crossly.

"PLEASE GIVE ME ONE MORE CHANCE"

Everyone was sitting in the log cabin in the garden, and there was only one small space left on the sofa next to Rihanna. I walked across and squeezed in. Penny said, "I know no one feels like having a meeting today, as you're all upset that Nancy has gone into hospital for a time. But when it's safe for her to be here with us again, she'll come back. Her parents are keen for her to have treatment here on the ward. But for now we need to talk about another matter. On the ward there is a very unhappy girl: Anna has told me that some of you are ignoring her. That you're angry because she's taken things from you."

"Nicked them," said Rihanna.

"And she tried to make it look like I was the thief," I said.

"Suzy and Rihanna, can you listen to what Penny has to say?" Fran said.

Penny went on. "Anna's very sorry about the distress she's caused you all."

"Not so sorry she wants to come to this meeting," said Rihanna sulkily.

"Rihanna and Suzy, that's because both of you are being horrid to Anna," said Penny, looking directly at both of us. "And she feels she can't face any more nasty comments from you in this meeting."

"Yeah, you girls have been really catty," said Wyatt. "When you get to know Anna, she's actually nice."

"You're just saying that because you fancy her," said Rihanna.

Wyatt's face turned scarlet. "Yeah, right. You were horrible to Nancy too. And now she's in hospital."

"Shut up! It's not my fault she's there!" screamed Rihanna. She was sobbing, and tried to stand up.

"Sit down, Rihanna," said Penny forcefully. In a softer voice, she said, "I know everyone's feeling upset, but I won't have any of you casting blame on Nancy. She's a very unwell little girl. She's been eating virtually nothing for several months. I know that each of you, in your own way, were friendly to Nancy when she was here, and anyway she was only with us for a very short time. And I'm sure that when Nancy returns, you'll all do your best to make her feel welcome."

In a brisker voice, she continued, "I wonder if you could all show the same consideration to Anna." There was a long, uncomfortable silence. Penny continued, "Anna's asked me to read out a letter that she's written to you all. But there's no point in me doing this if you're going to keep interrupting me."

I slumped down further in my seat. I was so sick of this place.

Penny started to read the letter.

"Dear everyone,

You'll now all know that I nicked stuff from a few of you, and I do really understand this has upset everyone. I can't blame you for not trusting me now. I would never normally nick stuff, but I was in a terrible place in my head. After coming here I was really upset, and felt I just had to binge on food and buy laxatives to get rid of it. This is what I took the money to buy. I was going to sell Rihanna's ring, and use the money to buy a train ticket home. If I'd known how important the ring was to Rihanna, I'd never have taken it. But luckily Penny found out before I could–"

"The bitch," snapped Rihanna. "Anyway, Penny, I thought she'd confessed this stuff to you? This letter makes it sound like you caught her out."

Penny carried on reading.

"I'm here like all of you, trying to get better. For me that means breaking the cycle of bingeing and getting rid of food. I've been caught up in this for five years. I'm in a lot of trouble at the moment. As well as nicking stuff in the clinic, I'm in trouble with the police for shoplifting. I promise that I will never nick stuff from any of you again. Please give me one more chance, and I promise that I won't let you down again.

Love from Anna"

"Is that it?" asked Rihanna.

"Yes, I think it's a letter that shows someone is

really very sorry," said Penny. "Don't you think so Fran?"

"Yes, definitely," Fran said. "I'd like you all to think about the fact that most of you, if you're honest with yourselves, did things when you first came here which you wouldn't do now, and regret."

"I didn't nick anything," said Rihanna indignantly. "And I didn't get the others to take chocolate from the clinic's store cupboard."

Penny's eyes were curious again, and she said, "Well, that's another issue that I'll need to deal with separately."

Penny went on, "So maybe you could all be kind and give Anna another chance? Why don't we have a vote on who's going to accept this letter as an apology – so it's an end to the matter?"

Wyatt's hand went up.

I hesitated. Into my mind came the awful picture of Anna with her bags packed, forced to leave. We'd take it in turns, to say goodbye to her, as we did when Leah left. But what would I say? Because I knew, didn't I, that Anna, like the rest of us, needed a second chance to get better. And who would give Anna another chance? I now put my hand up.

"And Rihanna? What about you?" asked Fran.

Rihanna reluctantly lifted her hand.

"Thank you, everyone," said Penny. "I'm sure Anna will really appreciate the fact that you're giving her another chance. We'd better stop there, as it's nearly time for lunch."

Everyone went through to the kitchen except for me and Rihanna.

"Why did you forgive Anna?" Rihanna asked me.

"Why not? Life's too short for going on about

that stuff," I said. "Why are you being weird with me?" I blurted out. "What have I done?"

She looked at me nastily. "What have I done?" she repeated, in a mocking voice. "You set me up so that Penny found out I was taking Turboslim."

"No, I didn't," I said quickly.

"Yes, you did...She came in and said as much. Apparently, you've been writing about me in your stupid diary."

I went crimson. "I'm so sorry...I'd no idea that she'd read my diary. Why didn't you tell me before?"

"Penny made me promise I wouldn't, when she searched through my things this morning," said Rihanna.

The door opened and Fran stood there. "Girls, what's the matter?" Neither of us said anything. "Well, come through for lunch, please."

Rihanna turned to walk towards the door, but as she went she glared over her shoulder. There was real venom in her eyes.

I felt frozen. *At least I could get away from her this weekend, as I had my Exeat weekend coming up.*

The road seemed to wind round the other houses in our street forever. Finally our car pulled into the drive. Mum switched off the engine. "Suzy, I'm so pleased you're here this weekend. Please try to make it a success."

I stared back at her. It was like she was suggesting it would be my fault if it didn't work out. *This wasn't much of a welcome!*

A minute or so later a smiling Rupert opened the door and Ben was letting off party poppers.

"Careful! Don't frighten her!" Mum said.

"He's not, Mum!" I snapped. I wished that she'd stop treating me like a fragile patient.

I walked into the house and there was an amazing blue cake lit with purple candles. On top was a girl done in icing, with long brown hair and a purple dress.

"Recognise her?" Ben asked.

"Yes, is that me?" I said, in astonishment.

"See if you can blow all the candles out," said Rupert.

So I took in a big breath and blew out all of the candles. Mum carried the cake away. *Probably, she was going to cut it up, and I'd be expected to eat a slice!* But I didn't want to look ungrateful.

"Ben, it was really sweet of you to bake the cake," I said.

"I can't take all the credit," Ben said. "Nick helped me. We baked it together, and he iced it. We figured if we make you nice cakes, you won't stop eating again. Nick wants you to phone him. He says he hasn't spoken to you for a few days."

"I'm about to ring him," I said.

"Promise?" Ben said.

"Yeah, sure," I said.

Mum came back through. "Molly has phoned too," she said. "She and Carla would really like to visit you this weekend. Why don't you fix something up?"

Mum must have been listening to my conversation with Ben, and I was annoyed. "I'll think about it," I muttered.

The doorbell rang, and Ben went to answer it. I could hear Molly and Carla's voices talking downstairs.

"Guess who's here?" Ben called upstairs.

I froze on the spot. *What if they didn't recognise me?*

I met Molly and Carla on the landing. They looked awkward, I thought. Perhaps there was silence for just a few seconds, but it felt like much longer.

Carla was the first to speak. "Suzy, it's great to see you again." And she hugged me.

"Yes, it's great," said Molly. "Let's have a group hug."

In my bedroom, Molly and Carla grinned as they watched me shake the present they'd given me.

"Give me a clue," I said.

"It's something you wear. But you can change it, if you don't like it," Molly said. "We've got the receipt."

I ripped off the paper. Inside was a size 12 satiny turquoise top, with silver sequins sewn onto it. "It's really nice," I said, surprised. *How did they know I was now a size 12?* "You know lots of my old clothes are too small now," I said.

"We should cut them up. Where are they?" Molly suddenly said.

"What?" I said, staring at her, feeling surprised.

"Have you got some scissors?" Molly asked, a smile on her face.

"Well...yes," I said, reaching for the pair on my desk. I walked over to my wardrobe and opened the doors. Most of my clothes were hanging in the wardrobe, nicely ironed, and sorted into different types.

"Let's start with that white dress," said Molly. "You were wearing that when you got tiny. On second thoughts, I think that you should do the cutting."

I took a small snip. I felt like I was doing something awful, but liberating at the same time.

"Go on, bigger snips," said Carla.

Bits of dress started falling round me. Soon the floor was covered with strips of fabric. There was a knock, and Mum poked her head round the door. I expected her to be furious that all these clothes were ruined, but she smiled and quietly shut the door. *Was she in on this as well?* I wondered, as I carried on snipping.

It felt a relief to be back on the ward. The last few hours at home had felt a real strain, as I kept worrying whether I'd jump through the final hoops, so that Mum could give a glowing report to Penny about the weekend. Funny that nobody seemed to be around. Walking down the next flight of stairs and turning the corner, I was pleased to see Wyatt. "How was your weekend?" I asked him.

"Haven't you heard? Nancy's died," he said.

I stared at him in horror. Neither of us said a word.

Eventually I said, "When did you find out?"

"Fran told the others at lunchtime, but I was out having pizza with my parents. Not really my idea of fun," Wyatt said, his face grim.

"Where's Anna?" I asked him.

"The games room, I think."

I walked down the stairs, then down the corridor. I couldn't quite believe the news about Nancy. I pinched myself a couple of times on the arm to be sure I was really here and not dreaming. As I approached the games room, I heard voices and my name was said. I stopped and listened.

"Do you think Suzy's really better?" said Anna. "It's easy to pretend, isn't it? And it's awful to think she could stop eating again, and end up like Nancy..." Her voice sounded choked up, like she was fighting back tears.

"She'll still worry about calories and stuff. Most people do – you know Yun did before she left," said Rihanna. "What d'you think, Anna? You share a room with Suzy?"

I cringed hearing them talking about me, but part of me was really curious too.

"I think she's nearly better," said Anna. "Sometimes you can tell she doesn't like looking in the mirror, but that's about all. If I'm honest, I'm quite jealous. I wish I felt like I was getting better, you know, inside, but I don't."

I left quietly and went back down the corridor. *At least Rihanna was being nice about me. I was relieved, because she'd been so angry when Penny had discovered my food diary. What's more, Rihanna and Anna were now on talking terms – maybe it was the shock of Nancy dying.*

I'd better phone Nick back. I didn't want him finding out second-hand from Ben, or maybe from Molly or Carla, that I'd met up with them this weekend.

In the kitchen, I saw that Fran's eyes looked red and sore. "I've been looking for you, Suzy. Your mum thought you'd be in your room. I'm afraid I've some very sad news to tell you."

"About Nancy?"

Fran nodded, looking really sad.

"Wyatt's already told me."

"It must be a big shock for you to hear this. Do you want to talk about the news?"

"Not really," I said. "I didn't really know Nancy. It just seems really young to die..."

"It is...anorexia can have terrible consequences. That's why it's important, Suzy, that you do your best to get well."

I now felt really awkward; remembering what I'd come to ask her, I said quickly, "Is it all right if I use the phone? I need to speak to Nick. You see, I didn't get to see him this weekend."

Fran smiled weakly, and said, "I'm afraid all the lines are busy. Why don't I give you your mobile back? Do you have enough credit to make the call?"

"Yes, I think so," I said, hardly believing that I was being trusted with my mobile, finally.

When I switched it on, quite a few messages popped up. *How was I going to explain to Nick that I'd avoided him this weekend?*

"Hi Suzy," he said, sounding quite miserable.

"You know when I rang you from home this weekend? Well, there was something I didn't tell you."

"What is it?" He sounded worried.

"Well, on Sunday I saw Molly and Carla. I felt I couldn't really face seeing anyone else, and it was a last-minute thing. I'm so sorry."

"I was expecting you to say that you didn't want to see me because there was some other cute guy." Nick laughed, but it sounded flat.

"Oh no, nothing like that. I just worry that you won't fancy me any more."

"I've told you, Suzy, you don't have to worry about that..."

I interrupted, and said, "Nick, I'm doing my best to recover, because when I came back to the ward tonight, I learnt that this nine-year-old who was here for a bit, and then went into hospital, has died. I don't want that to happen to me."

There was a long pause, and Nick said in a strong voice, "Don't worry, Suzy, it won't. You want to get better, and that really matters. And you've got me, Ben and Molly too to help you when you get out. That's if you'll let us."

My chest tightened, because I knew that for ages I'd been shutting everyone out, thinking that this was better. Now, I wasn't at all sure.

"Why don't we fix something up for next weekend?" Nick said. "You'll be home again, right?"

"Yeah, let's meet on Saturday – is that okay?"

"Come round for lunch."

"Okay, great," I said. "Bye, see you on Saturday."

"The moment of reckoning," said Penny, smiling at me.

I stared at the scales. *What if I had lost weight?* "I did eat all my calories this weekend. I promise," I said.

"Your mum told me you did. Look, I'll be happy if you've just managed to maintain your weight."

I stood on the scales. I was used to getting on and off them, but this time it felt far worse.

"You're at target," said Penny, looking at her clipboard. "Congratulations, Suzy!"

I was in shock, and stared at her. "But it's half a kilo over!" I blurted.

"That's only marginally over – your weight will always fluctuate around your target."

But I felt cheated. Accepting my target weight was hard enough, but weighing even more felt terrible.

"Many of our patients lose weight after discharge," said Penny, clearly meaning Leah.

"Oh, I'm sorry." It was all I could think to say. I thought it was unfair that she couldn't come back here for treatment. For anorexia's so compelling, and Leah was obsessed with getting skinnier. Just like Nancy had been... and look what had happened to Nancy. *What if Leah died too?*

Downstairs everyone looked fed up, waiting to get breakfast over with. I sat down, and couldn't help smiling.

"What is it?" Wyatt asked.

"I'm there – at target, I mean," I said.

Wyatt clapped me on the shoulder. "Told you it would happen. Well done!" he said.

I saw Rihanna scowling over at me, but I ignored her.

"How does it feel?" Leah asked.

"A bit weird," I said. "I'm kind of happy to be at target, and angry at the same time. Actually, I'm half a kilo over my target weight!"

Penny entered the kitchen, and I fell silent. She said, "I meant to tell you all that Nancy's dad rang me to say that he and Nancy's mum are very touched by the flowers you all sent for Nancy's funeral. They'll be coming back to the ward to collect Nancy's things, probably in a couple of weeks, and they'd like to thank you themselves."

"I still can't believe she actually died," said Anna.

"Well, it can happen, can't it," said Wyatt.

"I'm afraid that's true," said Penny. She cleared her throat, and said, "And now to move on to a completely different topic, some of you will be pleased to know there's a trip to the water park this afternoon. It's only for those of you who are at an appropriate weight to go on the slides. The rest of you have the newspaper group."

I smiled, because I was now allowed to do all the activities here.

"Cool. We'll go down the scariest slides," Rihanna said.

"Rihanna, I'm afraid you can't go," said Penny quietly.

"Why not?" shouted Rihanna. Her face had turned a furious shade of red.

"Rihanna, why don't we discuss it after the meal?" Fran said, who was weighing out the cereal.

"No, tell me now!" screamed Rihanna.

"We need to wait for those scars on your arms to heal first," said Penny.

She must have been self-harming again!

"They are healed," shouted Rihanna. "I hate it here!" She got up, knocking her chair over as she stormed out.

Fran followed after Rihanna. There was a knock at the door, and after a short pause, Elizabeth entered. "Sorry, I and the guys left behind a few bits. I just came to pick them up," she said.

I said, "We miss you guys! This place is boring now."

Elizabeth replied, "That's sweet of you. We miss all of you too."

"You'll be seeing them again," said Penny. "They're coming back next week for a dinner."

"Can we cook the dinner?" asked Anna.

"I don't see why not," said Penny. "What do you think, Elizabeth?"

"That would be wonderful," she said, and smiled enthusiastically.

I saw Anna and Wyatt exchange grins, as if they were thinking something up.

The others had gone up to bed. It was still quite early and I felt really wide awake.

It occurred to me that the others were probably water-tanking tonight. That was why they'd pretended to go upstairs to bed early.

Rihanna came in, with a sulky look on her face, and sat down. I carried on watching telly. An Amy Winehouse song was playing about being in Rehab, and Rihanna joined in. Her voice was okay, but the way she was pouting, you'd think she was going to be on X-Factor. As the song ended, Rihanna asked, "How did I sound?"

I said, "It was good. But don't you want to sing about things other than places like this?"

"Oh...aren't we high and mighty, now we think we're cured."

Suddenly I was sick of her sarcastic comments. I said, "Look, I didn't mean it that way. But is this all you want?"

She said, "Think you look good, now you've got a big bum and flabby arms?"

I stared back at her.

She went on, "I bet Penny and your mum tell you how good you look." She eyed me up, looking amused. "No one's gonna be honest, coz they don't want you restricting again. What's Nick gonna say when he sees his girlfriend looking chubby?" She was silent, but her eyes were mocking me.

"Shut up!" I screamed at her. "At least I have a boyfriend. You – you're a freak, you've been here for what it is it...a year? Everyone's given up on you, and any friends you did have will have forgotten you," I shouted.

"Yeah, right? I've got friends," Rihanna shouted. "And they don't do weird experiments, trying to change me from fatso-the-saddo into someone people like! It hasn't worked, has it!" She was laughing in my face.

I stared at her. *She could only know this if she'd read my diary!*

"I DIDN'T TAKE THOSE PILLS, I PROMISE"

None of us could concentrate on watching *Diary of a Wimpy Kid*, while the film crew were eating the dinner we'd cooked next door. Wyatt came back from the kitchen with a grin on his face, sat down on the sofa and put his arm round Anna.

"Go on, tell us," Rihanna said, sounding annoyed. "Are they eating the food?"

"Yes, even Elizabeth," Wyatt said. "They've finished the prawn cocktail and they're now onto the chicken curry. There's a whole carton of double cream in the curry."

We laughed. I suddenly noticed that this was the first time we'd laughed together since hearing of Nancy's death. "Have they noticed?" I asked.

"They don't seem to. Graham and David have said the curry is the best they've ever had. But then Graham must like fatty food with that big gut. They're drinking beers, too."

"Elizabeth can't be," said Rihanna.

"She and Penny are drinking red wine. That's got more calories in it than white wine."

I went back to watching the film. I could hear the new girl, Melissa, still crying. She was my age and had long curly blonde hair, which would have been pretty if clumps of it weren't falling out. Melissa had cried on and off ever since her parents had admitted her yesterday. I'd tried to cheer her up, as had the others. Now, there was nothing I could think of to say. I wished that Yun was here, because she'd been able to make people feel better when things were rubbish.

The door opened and Penny came in. "Is everyone okay?" she asked. "Elizabeth and the guys wanted me to thank you for the trouble you've gone to."

"When can we come through?" Rihanna asked.

Penny said, "After dessert, when we're having coffees. Elizabeth gave me the message to pass on that they've something to give each of you to thank you for taking part in the documentary. Apparently, they've been very impressed with your acting skills."

"Let's hope we get Oscars and money," said Wyatt, rubbing his hands together. Anna smiled.

"I don't know about that," said Penny, laughing. "But I'm sure it's something worth waiting for."

Mike came in, wearing a suit and silver tie which looked really smart. "Rihanna, can I have a word?" he said.

She got up from the sofa with a loud sigh, and I felt a wave of satisfaction. Lucky it's not me under the radar eye, I thought.

I checked the time. I could phone Molly soon, catch up on her news of orchestra and school. I found I wanted to know what was happening these days, now that I didn't have much longer here.

I was going to put the £100 we'd each been given by the film crew towards an iPad, but it was annoying that I had to wait until I went home to buy it. Penny was looking after everyone's money, in case they used it for something they shouldn't. Wyatt now entered the kitchen.

"Suzy, what've you chosen for your treat?" asked Wyatt.

"A trip to the circus would be good," I said. "It still feels weird I'm there at target, and celebrating getting out."

"Yeah, I hope they have contortionists," Wyatt said. "I'd really like to know how they bend like that."

Penny entered the kitchen with a furious look on her face. She was holding some packet, but I couldn't make out what the pills were. "Suzy, how could you cheat?" she shouted.

I stared at her, but I knew better than to say anything until I found out exactly what I was supposed to be guilty of. I didn't have to wait long.

"Fran, I've found laxatives in Suzy's cello case," said Penny.

I immediately thought of Anna - she must have hidden the laxatives there.

"Oh, Suzy. That's very disappointing," said Fran quietly.

"And these don't work, you know, Suzy," said Penny. "When they make you go to the loo, it's mainly water you're getting rid of."

I shouted, "But I haven't taken these pills. I promise."

"Penny said, "Sorry, I don't believe you."

"But I haven't. I'm not that stupid," I shouted. "Why won't you believe me? You always think the worst of me and it's not fair."

Fran said, "Suzy, you've got that wrong. Penny treats everyone here fairly. The thing is we've got a problem, because those laxatives have been found in your cello case."

"And so far you haven't given us a satisfactory explanation," said Penny.

"How can I? They must have been planted there by someone." I was going to say Anna's name, but Wyatt standing there stopped me. I had to have evidence that Anna had put the laxatives in my cello case.

"I'm not listening to this," said Penny. "Don't try to get one of the others into trouble for something you know you shouldn't have done."

"I didn't take laxatives!" I shouted.

Penny frowned. "I'm going to have to contact your mum to say you won't be able to go home this weekend."

I stared at her, shocked; then I started to cry. "You can't...I've made plans," I said.

"Well, you'll have to unmake them, won't you?" said Penny.

"Well, you look happy," said Wyatt, as he sat down on the sofa.

There was a long silence. I wanted him to go away. He was going out with Anna, so of course he was going to cover up for her.

"Look," Wyatt said. "For what it's worth, I don't think you took those laxatives, okay? And Anna didn't hide them in your cello case, if that's what you're thinking."

Wyatt must have been reading my mind.

Wyatt went on, "I've asked Anna about the laxatives, and she promised me that it wasn't her. I think it was Rihanna. But convincing Penny of that is going to be really difficult."

"Why would Rihanna do that?" I said quickly.

"Coz you snitched on her about taking Turboslim," Wyatt replied. "Now Penny won't let her have her own money in case she buys some pills."

"It's not my fault that Penny read my diary," I said.

"I see," said Wyatt, and he looked thoughtful. "Look, don't get down. We'll work something out."

"But now I'm not allowed home at the weekend," I said. "And the others are mad at me because the bathrooms are kept locked now. Every time I go, a member of staff stands outside. It's awful!"

"I imagine it is," Wyatt said. He gave a wry smile. "And if staff see you don't keep going – will they change their minds?"

"I doubt it," I said. "Fran's already said that they suspect the laxatives have already gone through my system. She's thinking that I really took them."

"Staff can be so stupid sometimes," Wyatt said.

I nodded, feeling glad that he was taking my side on this.

"Well, cheer up," said Wyatt. He punched me playfully on the arm, and went out.

I stared miserably at the wall. Then I went to find some paper and pen to write a letter to Nick. *What would he think now that I couldn't meet him this weekend?* I tried hard to think of a good excuse. Nearly anything was better than mentioning laxatives.

Ben skated beside me, the two of us going way faster than Mum, who stayed close to the barrier, as she was scared of falling over again. I felt quite nervous sliding over the ice. But at least Penny had let me come out with them, after Mum had pleaded with her.

"Hooray, we're there," I said, grabbing onto the barrier.

Ben grinned at me. I could see that he thought I was making a big thing of getting round the rink. He looked over his shoulder, and said, "I think Mum needs a break. Let's go and get a Coke."

"Okay," I said.

Mum had caught up with us now. She looked really flustered.

"We're taking a break from ice-skating," Ben said, and grinned.

"Glad to hear that. I'm tired," Mum said. She went on, "I've been thinking, Suzy" – and she looked carefully at my face – "If what you tell me is true, and you didn't take those laxatives..."

"I didn't," I snapped.

"Okay, don't shout," said Mum. "Well, I suppose I can try talking to Penny."

"It won't make any difference," I said. "She'll just say that I've manipulated you."

"Well, she can't disregard what I'm telling her as

well."

"Yes she can. And she will," I said stubbornly.

Ben said, "We need to think of a way you can frame that Rihanna."

"That's not going to help!" snapped Mum, going to get drinks for us all.

But it might! I thought. I wasn't sure what trap to set, but maybe Ben knew.

It was night, with a low moon above the trees, the first that I'd seen for ages, casting an eerie glow over the log cabin where Rihanna was with the Goths.

Meanwhile inside, my feet felt rooted to the spot. I didn't have the nerve to confront Rihanna.

Yes, I did, that was stupid. The lies Rihanna had made up about me being addicted to laxatives were terrible. She didn't want Penny learning any different, as then she'd lose face. But still, the thought of what I had to do now made my tummy churn alarmingly.

If everything went to plan, that was one thing; but there was the potential for so much to go wrong. And Rihanna's temper frightened me. Anna was helping me out tonight, because she wanted to frame Rihanna. Anna didn't want anyone thinking that she had taken those laxatives. She must have been sitting outside for some time with the Goths, and the voice-recorder hidden inside her pocket was recording everything. But was she going to manage to switch the topic to me?

Running down the stairs felt good. It felt like I was doing something at last. In the lounge Melissa was watching telly, and she called out to me. "Hey, do you want to play cards?"

"No, can't now," I said briskly.

I realised that Melissa was in the lounge because staff were doing checks on her, probably every fifteen minutes. Come to think of it, Anna and I were lucky that the checks being done on us were only once an hour, so we had time to confront Rihanna. Wyatt wasn't able to help, as he was at his school play.

Along the corridor, I could see Tommy, the night nurse, busy with paperwork in the office.

Slipping across the garden, I reached the log cabin. I could already hear the raised voices above the loud music. I looked in through the window.

"Rihanna, you think you're so clever," said Anna. "But, I reckon it's pathetic planting laxatives on someone who's about to be discharged. It's like you're jealous that Suzy's about to pick up her old life with her friends and family. It's like when you told Penny I was exercising in my room, because you didn't like the fact that I was going out with my family, and you weren't."

"Yeah, right," said Rihanna, smirking. She turned to the Goths, and said, "Suzy's this girl here who's a liar, and Anna's believed her."

"Really? I'd no idea," said Mel. "I guess it's the quiet ones like Suzy you have to watch out for." She laughed nervously, but looked uncomfortable. She topped up their glasses with neat vodka. Even Anna was drinking, probably to blend in.

"Yeah, you wouldn't believe some of the lies Suzy tells," said Rihanna. "She remembers them too, coz she writes her lies down in this stupid diary..."

Now was my moment!

"But they're not lies, Rihanna, are they?" I shouted, entering.

"What in hell?!" shouted Rihanna.

"Yes, get this straight, Rihanna, I know you planted those laxatives on me." I spotted her bag on the table, which the Goths must have sneaked in again. "I can bet what's in there." I grabbed the bag.

"Get off that – you bitch!"

Rihanna's hands were wrestling for the bag, and so were mine.

"Why do you care?" I shouted.

"Coz it's mine!" she screamed.

Rihanna's hands were scratching my face. I was worried about my eyes, and shielded them with my left hand. I'd nearly lost my grip on the bag, but Anna came to my rescue, trying to pull the bag away from Rihanna.

"Christ, you lot are making me nervous!" screeched Mel.

That was when the bag split open, and out spilled razor blades and needles, and loads of pills.

"See – there's the evidence," I shouted, staring at Rihanna. Her cheeks had gone bright red.

"What the fuck!" shouted Mel. "Are you a druggie, Rihanna – as well?"

"No, she uses the razors and needles to harm herself, don't you, Rihanna," I shouted.

"So what?" screamed Rihanna.

"That's gross!" said Mel.

"And we've been bringing you that stuff," said Ella, looking pale and shocked.

"Yes," I said. "And when Rihanna doesn't get her own way, she tries to frame other people with stuff. It's you, Rihanna, who put these laxatives in my cello case."

"No!" Rihanna yelled.

"Go on, admit it!" I screamed, staring her in the face.

"Okay, but it was just once," she said. "But you made it so that Penny found out about the Turboslim."

I turned to look for Anna. *Where had she gone...?*

Ella and Mel were trying to escape. "Look, we've got to make a move," Mel said nervously. "We don't want to turn into pumpkins."

"What about meeting tomorrow still?" asked Rihanna.

"I think we're busy," said Ella.

Rihanna was crying. "You weren't earlier." She moved so she blocked the doorway.

"What are you doing, you nutter?" shouted Mel.

"Look, don't believe what Suzy's said," Rihanna begged. "I told you she lies all the time."

Suddenly I was really angry. "That's crap you're making up, because you can't stand it that I'm actually more normal than you are. That I have a life to go back to."

"Shut up!" Rihanna shouted. She wheeled round to the Goths, and said, "I really need you to bring the other stuff. I promise I'll..."

"Promise what, Rihanna?" asked Penny, from behind her. I realised that Anna must have gone to get Penny and Tommy. Rihanna wheeled round, looking pale.

"Fucking nothing!" Rihanna screamed.

"Rihanna, you need to calm down," Penny was saying.

"Yes, now, Rihanna," said Tommy.

"No, why?" screamed Rihanna.

I didn't see what happened next. Maybe Rihanna tried to push Penny or something, but Tommy and Penny were restraining her against the wall.

Penny was looking into Rihanna's face, "If this doesn't stop now, Rihanna, you'll be taking a sedative. You've gone too far."

Rihanna started sobbing and cried out, "They've left me!" I looked round and saw the back door was open. Mel and Ella must have slipped through there.

"Yes, I see our trespassers have departed," said Penny sarcastically. "Well, I know one of their mums fortunately," she said.

I waited for her next move.

"So what explanation can you give me for tonight?" Penny said. "You realise that you lot are in loads of trouble."

Anna now appeared, and said, "Penny, we've got something you want to hear," and she passed Penny the voice-recorder.

JUMPING THROUGH HOOPS

Luckily Anna was helping me out in art therapy. I watched as she painted a red stripe on my papier mâché balloon. I wouldn't have had the patience myself. It was difficult stopping the brush from going wonky, and if your fingers were rough, you made a hole. This had happened to me twice already, but Anna was an expert at patching things up. She knew that I really wanted to make this a miniature hot air balloon, something to give Nick when I went home for the weekend. He had often talked about going up in a hot air balloon, and taking me.

Wyatt came in and said, "Nancy's parents are still here. I saw her mum crying in the kitchen with Penny, but somehow I reckon the visit has helped them."

There was a long silence. I hadn't even seen Nancy's parents. Not feeling I really knew Nancy that well, I hadn't wanted to go into the lounge where Nancy's parents were chatting to Penny. I now said, "Wyatt, why do you think the visit's helped?"

"I guess they see the rest of us getting better, when we're some of the worst cases," said Wyatt. "I overheard Nancy's dad saying to Penny that they want to raise money for the clinic."

"That's nice, isn't it?" said Anna, who looked tearful.

"Yeah, it's good when people care," I said.

Everyone looked thoughtful.

Wyatt's face brightened, and he said, "Has anyone seen Rihanna?"

"No," I said glumly.

"It's like she's got no limits," said Anna, "coz, Wyatt, you know Rihanna told Penny I was exercising in my room."

"Well, I don't think any of us realised how far she'll go," said Wyatt. "Rihanna told Penny that I'm going out with Anna."

"I'm sorry," I said. "Still, I don't know why Rihanna took it out on you. You were at your school play when all this happened."

"I tried to confront her about planting those laxatives in your cello case. She assumed that I'd told you my suspicions," Wyatt said.

"Like I couldn't work it out for myself?" I said, pulling a face.

"You know I've heard staff talking about sending her to a secure unit," said Wyatt. "It's not just what happened the other night. Apparently, she's been caught self-harming in her room several times recently."

So that was why staff kept doing checks on Rihanna!

Wyatt went on, "But I don't think even Rihanna deserves that." He looked thoughtful, and said, "I don't know if you know, but her dad used to beat her and her mum really badly."

"No, I didn't," I said. Suddenly I needed to have something to do, so I peeled the dried-up paint off the paintbrush. If things were different, Rihanna would have a loving family who'd help her to get well, and she wouldn't be facing months shut up somewhere because of her extreme behaviour. We'd never have fallen out, and she'd still be fun to be with.

Fran came into the room, saying, "Suzy, Joe wants to see you."

I'd forgotten about my therapy. "I was just going," I said.

"Good," Fran said, glancing at her watch. "Because if you hurry, you'll only be a few minutes late."

In our therapy session, Joe was focusing on something really uncomfortable.

Outside, one of the cats was meowing as it jumped up onto the wooden railing. I wanted to get up and let it in so I could stroke it. But Joe was wanting to move on.

"So, Suzy, where do you want to go from this point? Because you have a choice, you know."

"But I don't see how worrying about Rihanna affects my recovery."

"You seem to think that if Rihanna leaves here it's your fault. But it's not," said Joe, and paused. "Rihanna, has to look at her part in this. You're not responsible for her recovery, just as she isn't for yours. Right?"

"Yes, I guess."

"So, Rihanna has to decide she wants to change. And you need to be focusing on your own recovery. I imagine the next few weeks will be quite stressful – you have this weekend at home, then you'll be preparing to leave here."

"Yeah, I can't wait," I said. "It's awful to have been cut off from my real life for so long. You know I never wanted to be here. I kind of just got used to it...but now each day's really long and boring."

"Well, there's not much longer to go now," Joe said, smiling. "But you should be prepared for the fact that even happy changes can be stressful."

I remembered when Mum had married Rupert, and we went to live in a bigger house; and when I'd started playing the cello with the county's Youth Orchestra. Yes, both things had been really good, but took some getting used to. "Yes, I suppose that's true," I said slowly. "I haven't told you, tonight's my treat. Fran and Mike are taking some of us to the circus."

"Well," Joe said brightly, "that's something fun."

"Suzy, they're made of rubber," Wyatt said. He grinned at me from where he sat at the other side of Anna.

One gold-costumed contortionist arched backwards into a ball, as her partner placed her hands on her back and did a handstand, arching her legs over her head into the splits.

"They're so thin," murmured Anna.

I wanted to say, "Can't you just shut up about weight?" For tonight I'd been so busy watching the show that I'd forgotten about my anorexia.

"They're way more flexible than even dancers are," I said to Wyatt.

"I wonder what the next act's going to be," Wyatt said. "That's going to be a hard act to follow. But they've all been good so far."

"Yes, I know," I said. A man now came on the stage spinning incredibly fast in different shaped hoops.

I thought of all the hoops we'd all been jumping through. At that moment Wyatt said, "Rihanna would have really liked this. I guess she's missing out."

And my thoughts clouded over.

"But I don't want to be size 12," I shouted at Mum. I now wished that I hadn't agreed to come clothes shopping with her in Oxford.

"You can't be size 10 forever," Mum said. "That's anorexic thinking." She disappeared behind the curtain, and I could hear her saying, "Could you tell my daughter that she doesn't look fat in these trousers, please. She won't believe me." Then Mum was pulling back the curtain.

A shop assistant who was about twenty, with heaps of dark curly hair and nice make-up, said, "You look great, honest. I wish I had your figure."

I looked at her curves; she was quite big. I stared back at my own reflection in the mirror. I still didn't really like the way I looked. *Was the mirror tricking me still?* Penny had said that was what happened if you had anorexia.

Mum turned back to the sales assistant, and said,

"My daughter is recovering from anorexia."

My cheeks felt hot, and inside I was cursing Mum's big mouth. The girl smiled at me kindly, like she understood how much I was cringing inside. "Oh, sorry to hear that," she said. "But honest, you look good. I really mean it."

"Thanks for your help," Mum said. The girl smiled and disappeared behind the curtain. Mum turned back to me, and said, "There you go. What did I tell you?"

"Mum, please don't be so embarrassing," I muttered.

"I was just trying to help," said Mum. "So are you going to get these things?"

I looked at the jeans and the jumpers. "I don't know. I really want to use the money I got from the documentary for an iPad."

Mum thought for a moment, and said, "Well, how about I get these clothes for you as a present? You need some more clothes."

"Okay, thanks," I said.

And Mum scooped up the new things and went to pay for them.

"Normal Coke or the disgusting stuff?" asked Nick. But he was smiling. It was an old joke between us, Nick thinking Diet Coke tasted of nothing much.

"Diet, please," I said.

"I thought you'd say that. I bought you a bottle specially," said Nick, pouring me a glass.

I followed him out to the conservatory. It felt really snug in there, though it was raining outside. We sat down together on the wicker bench. I felt really awkward now.

Nick now spoke. "Suzy, I just need to understand something...why did you shut me out for ages, when you went into the clinic? Was it something I did?"

"No, nothing like that," I said. "It's just I hated myself so much when I went into hospital...that I thought it'd be better if you got a nice girlfriend, who had fewer problems than me. Actually, I kind of thought you would do that. And I didn't want to feel really hurt, so I thought it best if I distanced myself."

"I kind of see," said Nick. "But I'm not that easily shaken off. I still really want to be with you. And I'll be supplying you with chocolate bars if you lose any weight. I'm not letting you end up like that girl you told me about who died." He was looking directly into my eyes.

Remembering Nancy, I felt really sad and looked down at the floor.

"Look in there," Nick said. He passed me a bag of enormous Galaxy bars.

I laughed. "You remembered it's my favourite," I said.

"Sure did," he said. His arm went round me, and he kissed me on the lips, then again. *I must feel not the least bit skinny. Did it matter? I wasn't sure yet.* I ran my hand through his hair, it felt spiky, just the way I liked it.

"Oh, sorry to interrupt," said Clare.

I drew away quickly from Nick, my cheeks going a deep red.

"Suzy, I just wanted to ask, are you staying for lunch?" Clare said. "I can make lasagne - your favourite."

"Oh, sorry, I'm having lunch with Mum and Rupert. *What if Clare thought I was lying?*

"Not to worry, I'll make it another time," Clare smiled warmly. "It's great to have you round, Suzy. We've both missed you," she said, nodding at Nick, "and it's lovely to see you looking better."

"And tonight we've got the party," said Nick, grinning.

"It's going to be small, isn't it?" I said quickly.

"I think so," said Nick. "Molly's taking care of that." Clare had gone, so I was free to turn to Nick and kiss him.

I tried to see the faces through the purple and yellow balloons. Nearly the whole of Molly's front room was filled with them. "Welcome back, Suzy," Molly called to me.

Ben was blasting a tune on his mouth organ, and Molly and Carla were both hugging me. Adam and Gavin waved from the corner. It was good, too, how Molly had kept her word about not inviting extra people.

"I love the balloons," I said.

"It's cool, isn't it," said Molly. "The best bit will be playing Pinata. The donkey's in the doorway."

I looked up and saw the colourful paper donkey. *It must be stuffed full of sweets!*

Ben was blasting on his mouth organ, and we turned round. "Good. I've finally got you to listen!" he said. "Dinner's about to be served, so please take your places."

"The guys have done all the cooking," Molly said. "They've been watching Jamie Oliver cooking pizzas on the web, then copied."

I didn't tell her that I used to spend ages watching Jamie's cookery programmes too.

The table looked really pretty with the pink serviettes folded into fans. I sat down next to Molly. We were so busy chatting and laughing that it was like old times. Nick and Adam brought in two piles of pizzas: one with cheese, peppers and mushrooms on top, and the other with ham and pineapple.

"Don't worry," said Nick. "The meaty ones are for us guys, because we're growing."

I smiled as Carla passed me a plate. *Luckily the weeks on the ward had prepared me for eating things like pizza!*

We'd finished a runny but delicious trifle and were chatting at the table, when Molly's phone started ringing.

Molly looked down, and said, "Oh, it's Gemma. I don't have to take it," she said to me.

I didn't say anything. The phone had rung off now, but it beeped with a message.

"I'll see what she has to say," said Molly. And she held the phone up to her ear. Molly said, "Suzy, Gemma's really upset. Will you listen?"

"*Hi Molly, can you ask Suzy if I can come round?"* I could hear Gemma trying to suck up to Molly. *"I know you're having a party for her at yours...I feel terrible about having been a bitch to Suzy. I've got her some flowers to say I'm really sorry. Please can I give them to her?"*

"What does she want?" asked Ben.

"To come round. She's pleading on the phone," I said.

"So what?" said Ben quickly.

"Well, she sounds sorry," I said. But Gemma was so two-faced it was difficult to tell.

"What do you want to do about it?" asked Molly.

"Dunno really," I said.

"It's totally up to you," said Molly. She got up and put on some cheesy music. Molly and Carla started dancing. Molly called out, "Suzy, come and dance with us – well, only if you want to."

I had just started dancing when the doorbell rang and Molly went to get it. She came back with a surprised look on her face, and said, "Suzy, Gemma's here with the flowers. D'you want to see her?"

"You don't have to," Ben said quickly.

But after dealing with Rihanna, seeing Gemma again didn't seem so scary.

Gemma was standing there under the porch, drenched from the rain. Her make-up looked terrible and her hair and clothes hung from her, damp and limp. She blurted out, "Suzy, I'm so sorry for everything. But I guess there's nothing I can really say to put things right, is there? Here, these are for you." She passed me a bunch of red roses.

They gave off a gorgeous scent. It took a few moments for me to weigh up what to do. I said slowly, "I was really hurt – but not so much now."

Gemma smiled, and said, "So you don't hate me?"

"No, I guess not," I said. "The flowers are really nice. Thank you."

"So I'll be seeing you around at school, I guess?"

"Yeah, sure."

"Look, I'd better go. My mum's waiting in the car," Gemma said.

I saw the red Golf parked under the street lamp. Gemma looked happier as she walked down the drive and the car disappeared.

Tonight, I was the one having the fun for a change!

"YOU NEVER THOUGHT THIS DAY WOULD COME, DID YOU?"

It kind of felt like I had parallel lives going on: here I was, still in the clinic, counting down to day 87 when I'd be leaving, but already in my head I was at home. I was excited about visiting my grandparents again. Granny and Grandpa were so pleased that I was better. Wyatt was also excited for me that I was going home. But Anna pretended not to notice. Although she seemed to have stopped bingeing on food, the idea of getting to a normal weight was still really painful for her. Nowadays, I barely talked to Rihanna. She was having a lot of therapy with Bird Cage, and the rest of the time she was really withdrawn.

I was glad that the others seemed optimistic about their futures. Next term Wyatt was going to start boarding at his school. He'd return to the clinic during his holidays, as he now thought of it as being a home, having lived here for over a year. I knew that he'd been getting straight As in his A-level coursework. He was so bright, I reckoned that if he stayed on track with the eating, he'd probably end up studying somewhere like Oxford. Anna was going to live at her dad's when she left the clinic, and would sit her GCSEs in the summer. She was excited about looking round possible sixth forms where she could study Art and Design. Yun had been back to the clinic for a follow-up meeting. She was still at her target weight, and was about to take her driving test.

Sadly, we'd heard that Leah had lost more weight since leaving the clinic. I really hoped that she wasn't going to end up in hospital again.

There was a knock on the bedroom door, and Fran came in. She said, "I found these sketchpads of yours in the art-room. You'll want to take these home, won't you?"

"No, it's all right. I'll leave them here for the others," I said.

"That's nice of you to think of the other girls, Suzy," Fran said, smiling. "Oh, and Rihanna also asked me to tell you that she wants to talk to you. I think she feels very sorry."

"So why doesn't she tell me that herself?" I asked.

"I think she finds it difficult to express how she feels."

"It's not that hard," I muttered.

"But you have the cello to help you express your feelings. Rihanna doesn't have that. She stores everything up inside. Please will you just speak to her?"

"Okay," I said.

As I went into Rihanna's room, she was sitting on her bed, painting her nails a deep purple colour.

"What's up?" she asked in a flat voice.

"Nothing much. Nice colour," I said.

"Yeah, it's all right, isn't it?" she said, looking at her toenails. "Look, Suzy, the other night when I said all that stuff, I was mad, right?" She stared at me, looking lost. "This place, when you've been here as long as I have, makes you go mental. I didn't mean any of it."

"And the Goths – what about them?" I asked.

"They're just weird," Rihanna said. "They've done a disappearing act on me – they obviously can't cope with a nutter."

"You're not a nutter."

"I must be," she moaned. "It feels like I've worn the anorexic T-shirt forever – and now Bird Cage has told my parents that I've got other problems as well. I reckon she's going to stick more labels on me."

"That's really annoying," I said. I remembered the advice Joe had given me soon after I'd been admitted here. "Remember that anorexia's just some label a doctor's made up. What matters is how you feel."

"But I just feel so empty inside. Like I'm a nobody."

"Well, you are someone," I said. "You've got more opinions than I have about stuff. You're someone who is always at the centre of a group, rather than on the outside, like I often am. And you're not going to a secure unit now, that's what you told Wyatt. So you can get better here. Probably, you'll be out quite soon."

Rihanna smiled and said, "Maybe. But this time I want to stay out. In the meantime, maybe I can find labels for staff. What about Penny who's a control freak? There's got to be some label for that."

So we'd made up a bit.

Joe's grin was really wide, but I didn't get why he was so amused.

I said, "But I only need to work out why the girls at school get so mad with other people, so that I don't upset them again."

"You're doing it again," Joe said.

"What do you mean?"

"Listen to what you've just said."

I repeated my words in my head again. *Don't upset the other girls.* It was like I was still scared of what they thought of me! I said, "But, I told you that I confronted Gemma the other day."

"Exactly," said Joe. "You're much stronger than you think you are. Just look at the enormous mountain you've climbed in the three months that I've known you. When you came here you were so underweight that it threatened your health, and now you're a healthy, attractive girl who can enjoy life again."

"I guess."

And you know what you need to do to stay well?"

I nodded. *It was good the list we'd worked out together: it included the triggers to avoid low self-worth, not overloading myself with goals to achieve, avoiding big arguments...*

"And Penny will refer you for some therapy near where you live," Joe said.

I nodded.

"So how do you feel about today being our last session?"

"Quite sad," I said. "You've helped me so much. Oh, I've remembered, I've got you a present." I passed it to him and watched as he ripped off the paper.

"Stress-balls, excellent," said Joe, squeezing one of them.

"It's for when patients like me stress you out."

He laughed, and then turned more serious. "Suzy, you haven't stressed me out. I've enjoyed working with you, and I think we've covered important ground together."

"I know. Thank you for everything," I said. "Well, I'll be going now."

"Bye, Suzy," said Joe.

As I walked down the corridor, I felt sad that therapy was over, but cheerful at the same time. No one had changed things for me like Joe had done. He had helped me to see how life could be so much better.

"You never thought this day would come, I expect, did you, Suzy?" said Penny.

I shook my head, and stared at the breakfast table where the others were sitting.

"Melissa and Anna, you weren't here when Suzy first came here. But in her early days here, as I'm sure Suzy will tell you herself, she found it very difficult. Over the weeks she's made amazing strides. Suzy looks really good now, I'm sure you'll agree."

There was an awkward silence, and Fran said, "Yes, you've done very well, Suzy."

"Yes, it's wonderful to see," said Mike.

Tears welled up into my eyes, and I bit my lip.

"Here's something to remember us by," said Fran, passing me an oblong present, wrapped in black and silver striped paper. Then everyone applauded. It was a special moment, for this was a tradition on the ward.

I suddenly felt sad, thinking that Yun and Leah weren't here to share my special moment. I tried shaking the parcel, but I couldn't work out what it was.

Wyatt had a go then, "Maybe it's a bomb," he said.

I laughed, as Rihanna said, "No, it's not! Go on, open it, Suzy."

I ripped off the paper, and inside was a silver Parker pen, with some refills.

"It's because you're always writing, Suzy," said Penny. "We thought it would come in useful."

I stared at the pen, a bit baffled. I'd hated it so much when Penny had read my diary without my permission. *Didn't she get that?*

"Right, let's start breakfast," said Penny.

Wyatt said, "Suzy, your last morning of Penny's breakfast. I'm sure you won't miss it."

"No, not one bit," I said, eating a mouthful of boring nut clusters. I saw Penny looking at me, and worried that she'd think I wasn't better enough to go home. I added quickly, "It's just at home I can eat my favourite cereals."

"What will you choose?" asked Anna.

"Muesli," I said, thinking that Penny couldn't say anything to that. Muesli had lots of calories in it.

A few minutes later, there was a knock and Mum popped her head round the door. "Good morning, Suzy, I was expecting you'd be finished," she said.

"Rupert's parking the car ready to start loading your stuff."

"I nearly am," I said, drinking some orange juice. "Anyway, I've started packing."

"Well, don't rush!" she said. I could tell that she was grateful that these days I actually did eat.

But a short time later, when we were upstairs, Mum got angry. "I thought you said you were nearly packed," she shouted. "This room looks like a bomb's hit it."

As I'd figured that all the drawers had to be emptied anyway, I'd tipped them up over the carpet. Now I felt upset, and replied, "Please don't have a go at me. I've been here for months. This day's supposed to be special."

Mum looked guilty, and said, "Sorry, Suzy, let's start again, shall we? I'm so pleased that you're coming home with us – these months have been awful for me."

And me! I thought.

Mum continued, "I want us to have a good relationship and be friends again, and not argue any more." She gave me a hug.

"I'm sorry about being horrible to you for ages. I just didn't want to be here," I said.

"Thank you for telling me that, Suzy. That means a lot to me," said Mum quietly, and her lip quivered. "We'll just take the last few months as having been a blip, shall we?"

Blip! My anorexia had been way more than that! Anyway, I'd changed so much and become more independent as well.

We started to pack my things, but after just a minute or two, I could tell Mum was getting annoyed. "Look, we're treading on each other's toes," she said. "Why don't I pack for you? And you go and say goodbye to the others?"

"Yes, okay," I said, feeling grateful.

I went out, and on the stairs met Wyatt. "So don't I get a hug then?" he asked.

"Yeah, of course," I said. I hugged him and grinned. "Thanks for everything. You've done so much to keep me cheerful, so I got through all this."

"Just glad to see you're better," he said. "Don't take this the wrong way, but I don't want to see you back here, as that'll mean you've lost weight. And you don't have to be like the rest of us, in and out of these places."

I knew who he was thinking of – Rihanna and Leah. And they'd actually survived – unlike Nancy. I didn't want to suffer like them. Wyatt smiled at me, and carried on up the stairs. I then made a decision, standing on that stair. *I'd try my best to stay well.*

Now I just had to say my other goodbyes, and I'd be free to go. I felt so sad that Wyatt didn't think he was getting better. Suddenly I felt the urge to walk round the ward one last time. I had to fix it in my mind for ever.

PART 3: RECOVERY

April 2013

WHAT ARE RULES, ANYWAY?

I was sitting in the lounge, practising my cello – Debussy's Sonata in D Minor. I was learning it with my new teacher at the Royal College, for a concert there in May. Julia and Michael were going to come and hear me. I looked at the music again. It was supposed to be about the clown Pierrot, with his white face, funny clothes, and white shoes singing to the moon, all alone. Before my anorexia I couldn't have known how that felt. It was the calorie counting, and the terror of discovery, which made me draw into myself, trusting absolutely no one. Then there were the months on the ward...

Mum came to the door. "Suzy, you need to pack up the cello. I want to serve dinner shortly."

"Okay," I muttered.

Why did she still boss me about? She always treated me like I was a little kid. Rupert did that too, sometimes. They often checked up on what I was doing, and were always reminding me that I needed to eat my 2,000 calories each day. Now I'd lost three kilos, that was even worse. It was like they were convinced that I was anorexic again. A relapse, they called it, as if it was an illness like cancer. But they didn't stop to think that it had something to do with them arguing all the time.

Rupert came in, holding his empty glass. "Come on, Suzy. Can you get a move on?" he said abruptly. "Your mum's already asked you once to put your cello away."

Since Rupert got made redundant in February, he'd been really snappy. I was quite worried by this, for I didn't like seeing him unhappy. Over the years he'd been with Mum, he'd tried his best for all of us, and sometimes all the arguing made me think that they might split up, which would be a real shame. I hadn't got anywhere with finding my real dad either. I'd spoken to my dad's brother on the phone, but he hadn't had any contact with my dad for years, and didn't know where he was.

Mum carried in the tablecloth and cutlery. "Suzy, will you lay the table?" She was looking really stressed.

"Okay Mum," I muttered, taking the things from her.

Mum had just fixed an appointment with Penny in the clinic for me to get weighed, so she was totally interfering.

"Well, if you put the weight back on," she said, "you won't have anything to worry about, will you?"

But it's not that simple! Penny would want to know why I'd not stuck to everything that was agreed when I got discharged. But November felt a long time ago, and anyway why should I have to stay the rest of my life stuck at target weight?

Mum went on, "Penny will probably tell you what I've said, which is that you shouldn't have given up the therapy she arranged for you."

"No, she won't," I said, glaring at her. But secretly I knew that she was right. "Anyway, I don't want to go to the family centre for therapy. It's opposite the school gates, so anyone can see me going in there."

"Well, we can find you somewhere else to go, even another therapist for you to see. Would that help?"

But it wouldn't be Joe! Oxford was too far away to have him still as my therapist. And therapy just wasn't the same with somebody else. "No, I don't want any more therapy!" I snapped.

It was running round my mind that I had to do something. Thoughts of dieting kept crowding in on me.

The documentary about Orange Tree Ward was playing, but I could barely look at it. Even though it was a school night, Molly, Carla and Nick had come round to watch. Ben was here too. We were having chicken fajitas that Rupert had prepared for us. I placed a small forkful of chicken on my wrap, and spooned loads of vegetables on top to make it look quite big, so no one could say anything. I thought that I looked chubby in some of the shots. *The camera adds ten pounds, people say. But what if I actually looked like that?*

There's Yun and Rihanna in the film smiling, like they're enjoying themselves. But were they really, or just acting? Kilo after kilo we'd all put on, each of us hating the changes that we saw in our bodies. All of the others were living at home, too. I hadn't spoken to, or messaged, any of them for ages – for keeping in touch just felt too painful, too much of a reminder of my time in the clinic.

"It looks like a nice place," Carla said.

"Yes," agreed Molly. "I'd love to be able to eat all those gorgeous desserts." The film was now showing me and the others sitting round the table, eating massive portions of chocolate cake.

"And no school or homework," said Molly, smiling brightly.

"Yeah," said Nick. "I hate coursework!"

How could they understand what it really felt like there?

Only Ben didn't say anything. He looked quite upset, I thought.

"Suzy, can I speak to you for a minute," Mum came in and interrupted the film. She sounded anxious, but not angry, so I couldn't be in trouble again.

I got up from the sofa, and went out to the kitchen.

"I just wanted to check you're all right watching the film, and it's not upsetting you," Mum said.

Mum and Rupert were watching the film in the study.

"No, I'm fine," I muttered and went back to join my friends again.

That sounded like footsteps outside my door. But Mum and Rupert were out at a lunch party, so it could only be Ben. He opened the door without knocking and barged in. I pushed down the cover of my laptop, pretending I'd logged off.

He didn't say anything, just opened the laptop and immediately restarted it. There was Rihanna's Facebook page, with postings from her friends who were also on diets.

"Why am I surprised?" Ben said.

"About what?" I said defensively.

"About you reading a bunch of diet tips like these." He now read out from the screen: "Make ice pops with Diet Coke. Eat tissues, they fill you up. Mmm...sounds really healthy!" he said, sarcastically.

"Are you going to tell Mum?"

He looked like he was thinking. "Aren't you going to tell her?"

"Why?"

"Because last summer the anorexia got such a hold on you, you nearly died," Ben said, his eyes fixed on mine.

I couldn't answer that one. I just stared back at him.

Sometimes I wanted to go on the pro-ana sites, but something stopped me. I think it was fear that I would get caught up in the old thinking again, when I kept obsessing about calories and skipping meals. I didn't want to end up dead like Nancy. I was scared that *litebitetara* had also died, because I hadn't heard anything from her since before I went into hospital.

Also, I listened to Penny and found a new therapist called Katie. I liked going to her house: in her office there was a painted elephant on the floor, and a really relaxed atmosphere, which made me feel that I could talk about my problems. So I told her how I found it difficult to deal with my mum's pressure, and how I didn't really like feeling on the edge of the in-group. I knew that Molly really liked me, so did Carla, and Gemma was nice to me these days. But I knew that she could be two-faced, and I worried that she would be bitchy again. I was still going out with Nick, and he had been a massive help through all this. I really cared about him, and I knew that he felt the same way about me. Still, sometimes when he put his arm round me or held me close, I worried that he found me chubby. I didn't like how my body was now much curvier than before, because I'd been made to gain all that weight.

Sometimes I thought of my anorexia as being a parrot on my shoulder, saying "Don't eat!" in my ear. I had to choose to ignore it. It was easier to do that when I was busy with fun things like playing the cello in the orchestra at the Royal College. We were learning Beethoven's 9th Symphony, and the rich chords lifted me out of myself. But when I was facing difficult things like my grandpa having a stroke, so that he got out of breath when he went for a short walk, I wanted to focus on calories again as a way of having some control. That was when I used the coping strategies that Katie had taught me, like sticking to my meal plans, and finding ways to relax that weren't exercising in my room. I found that going to a film with friends helped, or taking our new dog for a walk. She was a chocolate Labrador called Ella. I loved Ella; she was always pleased to see me, and really affectionate. I called her after Nutella, the chocolate spread. Secretly I liked chocolate, but I hadn't dared admit that when I was on the ward.

Mum got Ella so that I would have company in the house after school, as I now came home instead of going to my grandparents' house. And Ben would be going to Uni soon.

I knew that I wanted to stay well, as there was so much that I wanted to do with my life. Getting ill again would get in the way of that. Anorexia wasn't my friend, even though sometimes I thought that I'd be happier if I were thinner. That was why I wanted to tell you my story, so that it might help someone out there who is struggling with the food parrot sitting on their shoulder telling them "Don't eat!" I know that I couldn't have recovered on my own. I needed to talk to my friends, and tell Nick what was going on for me. That's why I'd suggest that if you're struggling with what I've been through, you talk to your friend, or your mum, or maybe a teacher. There is help out there.

FIVE YEARS ON

These days I feel lucky that the obsession with restricting my food intake isn't there most of the time. Seeing Tasha sometimes around Uni brings it all back: the calorie-counting, the need to wear clothes you hide behind and the constant fear that your friends are going to put pressure on you to eat. Tasha's chiselled face and glassy stare are so much like Nancy's were those days before she died. And Nancy faded out of existence all together. So, it's so sad to think that Tasha won't eat.

I'm not saying that recovery is easy. It can be really hard to carry on eating three healthy, nutritious meals each day and some snacks on top, when I sometimes feel upset or angry about the way things have gone. But way back when I was fourteen, and just a few months out of the clinic, I knew that the anorexia would destroy me if I didn't fight it. So I did.

AUTHOR'S NOTE

I had anorexia, then bulimia as a teenager. This novel is loosely based on my personal experience of descending into anorexia, and my treatment when I was aged fourteen in a specialist unit in London for children and teenagers' eating disorders. I went on to recover from my eating disorders when I was in my late teens.

My eating disorder led to me being interested in researching illness. After studying English at university, I went on to study for a Master's in Medical Humanities, and then gained a PhD in health geography. I have always had a passion for creative writing; I write a blog, which you can read on my website: www.mindmatters.store. *Size Zero* is my first novel for teenagers. In my down time, I enjoy playing the cello, like Suzy does in this novel.

Dr Roz Austin

Oxford

Instead of visiting pro-ana websites, please contact *Beat (beating eating disorders)*: helpline 0808 801 0677; youthline 0808 801 0711; website https://www.b-eat.co.uk/
See also NHS Choices Information:
www.nhs.uk/conditions/eating-disorders/d

Discussion points

1. Why did Suzy go on a diet?
2. Suzy was very worried about *litebitetara* whom she'd met on a website, because she stopped replying to her messages. Why do you think Suzy was worried?
3. Why do you think Suzy hid her weight loss from her friends and family for so long?
4. Describe Suzy's relationship with her boyfriend Nick, and her brother Ben. How do they react to Suzy's anorexia? How do they try to help her?
5. Suzy's mum said to her "Sorry, Suzy. I don't know how to get you to eat any more. But Dr Avery and Penny can help you." Suzy does not feel that she is ill enough to have treatment at the clinic. Do you think that Suzy's mum was right to admit her to the clinic?
6. What do you think are the key signs of anorexia? What are the risks involved in having anorexia?
7. In the clinic, Suzy makes friends with Wyatt and other girls who also have eating disorders. Was it helpful to Suzy at the time? Would it be helpful to Suzy in the long term, as her attitudes changed?
8. Suzy was given a food diary by Gemma. Gemma writes a letter to Suzy to say that she is sorry that she gave her this. Do you think that Gemma is genuinely sorry?
9. Rihanna said, "It's not because of models that we get anorexic, is it?" Do you agree with Rihanna? Or do you think that seeing size 0 models puts a

lot of pressure on girls like Rihanna and Suzy to aim to be size 0?

10. Why do you think Suzy is nervous about appearing in the documentary?
11. Do you think that Rihanna should have offered Suzy Turboslim (slimming pills)?
12. Why is Suzy encouraged to play the cello at the clinic?
13. Leah, the dancer, doesn't want to reach her target weight. Do you think that Suzy is right to be worried about Leah going home before she reaches her target weight?
14. Suzy's therapist Joe said to her, "Getting teased is something you're already imagining will happen. It may not." Do you think that Suzy's class's attitude towards her will have changed, now that she has had treatment in the clinic?
15. Suzy's brother Ben catches her reading diet tips on a pro-ana website, after she has come home from the clinic. Why do you think Ben is worried? Do you think Ben should tell Suzy's mum that she has been on this website?
16. After reading this book, do you have a better understanding of anorexia?
17. What do you think are the main causes of anorexia or bulimia?
18. Have you ever had anorexia or bulimia? How did this eating disorder affect your life?
19. Who would you reach out to for help if you were concerned about a friend, or you needed support yourself?

Printed in Great Britain
by Amazon

36391317R00158